Fake-out #1:
Human potential is dependent on circumstances

Fake-out #2:
The illusion of limits is our enemy

Illusion is an old friend who teaches us humility and eventually helps us fine-tune our connection with the mystical force behind it all.

"God works in mysterious ways" doesn't quite cover it. "We're all part of something bigger than we can understand" doesn't cover it. *The Big Fakeout The Illusion of Limits* does—in magnificent, easy-to-understand detail.

According to Henion, "Fake-outs are the framework behind the divine structure of life." He illustrates their importance with personal and historical stories. Then, lays out the hidden order behind human existence like blueprints on a table, making our perception of barriers irrelevant, and our age-old enemy of illusion-induced error as a rite of passage, which empowers us with a profound perspective.

WHAT AUTHORITIES ARE SAYING ABOUT *THE BIG FAKEOUT*

"*The BIG Fake-out—The Illusion of Limits,* 'wowed me!' It was spiritually moving, and inspiring. It had engaging stories anyone can relate to. This book will help the reader begin to look at the challenges of life calmly from a Higher Perspective and take the steps necessary to clear out the illusions that seem limiting. Mistakes are all part of the Divine Design of life and all decisions are good and have a purpose. Hunt Henion suggests we bless everyone, good and bad, follow our heart, and leave the fear and negatives behind. When we do, we will be vibrating as Love, Harmony, Gratitude and Grace. Henion says, as we come to know our Oneness with God and each other, we will evolve into the 'Homo Luminous' beings we were intended to be in this Age of Aquarius"

Rev. Abigail Albert of the Family Spiritual Center,
Poway Interfaith Team, and Board member
of the Affiliated New Thought Network.

"This book illustrates the fact that we tend to stumble through the drama of human life accepting the illusion of separation and limitation as reality. It brings the light of truth to the reader that all those "stumbling blocks" that appear to our conditioned mind as negative events are really stepping stones that can motivate us toward our true nature as spiritual beings with unlimited potential. The author has given the reader a book that is enjoyably inspirational."

Dr. Angelo Pizelo, President of the
Emerson Theological Institute and board member
of the Affiliated New Thought Network

"A very informative and interesting book…as individuals we try to control everything to get what we want instead of looking for truth and guidance…Do we even know who we are or where we are going? I found *The BIG Fakeout* by Hunt Henion to be very interesting and an intense read."

Carol Hoyer, PhD,
for Reader Views

"A unique sort of self-help spirituality manual,…utterly fascinating."
James A. Cox, Editor-in-Chief,
Midwest Book Review

"Hunt Henion performs literary alchemy, transforming everyday struggles we all endure into golden inspiration."

Lisa Shiel, award-winning author
on the paranormal

Also by Hunt Henion

The Don Q Point of View
Looking, Seeing, & Knowing

Shift Awareness Books
www.ShiftAwareness.com

The
BIG
Fakeout

The
BIG
Fakeout

The Illusion of Limits

Hunt Henion, PhD

Shift Awareness Books
for a BETTER Perspective!

Edited by Veda Henion

Book design by Five Rainbows Services

Printed in the United States of America
First edition, printed 4/2009

Shift Awareness Books
www.ShiftAwareness.com

To New Thought affiliated organizations everywhere

Acknowledgements

Danna's channeling has brought answers that have become the framework of all my writing. Her deep, abiding love brought me back from the brink, and renewed my run at life. She really has made EVERYTHING possible.

After meeting Danna, Veda, daughter number one, had her inner experiences verified and quickly developed a permanent connection to friends/family/guides from the other side. She's been a tremendous help as a ready source of quick answers, and the deepening love of this kindred soul has been a constant comfort.

Noel, daughter number two, whom I knew was sent to help me the day she was born, has been a life saver for all of us. I was told in channeling that this little angel actually hails from the dolphin world, and her unwavering playful optimism has been a rock in an otherwise often tumultuous sea. Hugging my little rock has been a blessing, which I appreciate more every day!

Dale, my son, and the man I am most proud of in the entire world: You were there when I first started looking for a reason to stick around, and living vicariously through your many successes growing up has renewed my hope. You are your own person, but your life is as close to me as my own.

Thank you, family! I know now, that without each of you and your love, I wouldn't even be here today.

Contents

Introduction

You need to claim the events of your life to make yourself yours. When you truly possess all you have been and done, which may take time, you are fierce with reality.
                                        –Flonda Scott Maxwell

As I've stumbled through life, I've been faked-out at probably every major turn, and tripped over every major stumbling block. Suddenly, this stumbling, falling, crawling journey has run me head-on into a fierce realization: These fake-outs weren't mere incidental inconveniences. I now know them to be the strands out of which the tapestry of life is woven and key in motivating us to our highest potential.

Life's little fake-outs are but fragments of the big illusion under which we all live. Our limited perceptions, misguided missions, and all the wrong ideas, which somehow get stuck in our heads are actually our Holy Grail on our quest to test our limits. Ancient wisdom, known to all the amused bystanders who carefully stay out of harm's way on "the other side of the veil," but forgotten to almost everyone living within the earthly arena, is that nothing here is what it seems. When the divine path winds all the way down to the physical realm, it rarely leads where we expect it to go, and life simply becomes a process of elimination as our hopes and goals get refined, and we get increasingly resourceful. We realize what doesn't work anymore, or maybe what never worked, and move on one step at a time.

Saviors have demonstrated how the twin virtues of detachment and love can take some of the wrinkles out of this process. However, in the end, the game plan's the same. We each agree to play a particular part, oblivious to other perspectives, in order to learn a particular lesson. Our higher self sits in a safe place, far away from the consequences of this fake-out world, and puts those lessons together lifetime after lifetime. We check in with that divine self between adventures, but generally never see that compiled picture of ourselves until after we've left our little, fragmented lives.

Everyday fake-outs are simply the map to our spiritual education this side of Eden. Following this map is a journey of hope and disappointment, love and loss, life and death. Where the road leads is always a mystery. It may take us across the mined battlefield. Or, when life is good, we're presented with surprises and choices all wrapped up like pretty little presents on Christmas.

Through trial and error, we unwearyingly unwrap the ones that look best and play with our new toys. Sometimes we get hurt. Sometimes we hurt others, or destroy the house! Whatever happens, we're blessed with the tormenting enlightenment of hindsight and a good guess about what to do differently next time.

That's the divine plan and one of our holiest of trinities: We're faked-out. We make mistakes. Then (hallelujah!), we learn and evolve.

Like ocean currents, order persists despite what's happening on the surface. What we perceive as the order may change from time to time, usually just when we feel we have a grasp on things. Still, beneath the surface, there's a beauty we usually can't even imagine. It's a strange and wondrous world where some sort of divine order constantly recreates itself out of the chaos of human error, ignorance and weakness.

I beg the weaver of the dualistic world's pardon as I step out of my contracted envelope of ignorance long enough to observe this ancient, secret plan. It's with great respect for the plan behind the sacred rite of falling victim to fake-outs that I admit that finding myself misled is getting a little old, and a new thought is emerging. The deluded and conflict ridden path of physical attachments has led me to an appreciation of peace and the simple joys of life. Also, from where I sit precariously perched out of harms way for now, I can see that I'm part of something bigger and much grander than the irritating, sometimes devastating, fake-outs at hand.

As I sift through the rubble where I've played and worked, I find that all the really important blessings in my life came about as incidental byproducts of what I thought I was doing. I'd continuously make mistakes, but somehow the universe healed them, so the wrong direction became the right one. I now know that some of those wrong turns were actually part of my prelife contract. Others weren't, but they still helped built my motivation for success and stimulate my creative approach to the constantly changing illusion of limitation.

Success over our challenges is often slippery to hang onto. However, no matter how "bad" things sometimes turn out, blessings have always been born from my disappointments. Disappointments have been plentiful, so I've been very blessed! I don't know exactly what they all are yet, but when I watch carefully, I can see them twinkle on the dark horizon. When I listen carefully, I can hear their music over the background noise of my crashing hopes. I've also watched over the years with amazement as these blessings have matured and blossomed with multifaceted personal benefits, even as the disappointments that gave them birth have died.

That's why I'm digging up all my old stuff and chronicling the discoveries like an archeologist going through ruins. Bear with me as I pick through the trash of my life looking for buried treasures. We'll sit in the dirt, discuss the finds, and maybe together, we can decipher which way is up in this upside-down world!

*To New Thought and Unity
of both worlds*

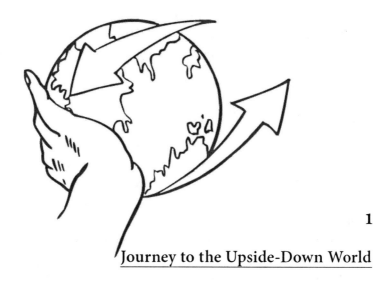

Journey to the Upside-Down World

There I was, standing around on a beautiful day. They were all beautiful days! I was chatting and laughing with my cronies, when someone came around asking for volunteers. Of course, I immediately spoke up.

"Do you remember what it was like? You sure you want to do this?" my friends instantly chimed in.

"Oh, yeah, no problem."

I don't remember exactly what I was volunteering to do, but I remember feeling totally qualified to do it. I think that's the last time I ever felt that way.

No one else in our little group volunteered to join me. So, I walked alone out of the land of perpetual light and love, peace and harmony. I jumped down into the darkness and woke up not knowing what was going on.

Now, after over a half a century here, I've come to the conclusion that none of us mere mortals really ever know what's going on. Sure, some think they do some of the time. However, at best, what we know is upside down. What we usually think is important isn't. What we usually think of as "bad" isn't, and what we see as the limit beyond which we can go no further is often just a new beginning. Still, we often live in a place where the upside of this upside down world is entirely invisible!

I came into this world head first, yelling and screaming, and everyone thought that's the way things were supposed to be. My warmth and comfort were suddenly stripped from me, and they were smiling as if everything was fine. I knew right away that something was wrong with these people.

I had just come from a world where everyone understood my every thought and feeling. Suddenly, I couldn't make myself understood at all about anything! They couldn't hear me; they couldn't see me. They thought they saw me, but all they were looking at was my poor excuse for a body. Everything that mattered seemed suddenly invisible, unreachable and ignored by everyone, and fifty plus years later, my waking life still looks just as upside down.

Many have written about the upside, with hope and promises that often just don't have the enduring ring of reality. We like to think these visions and attitudes will save us from the world of the conflict and mundane concerns. Unfortunately, many of us eventually wake up from our blissful Sunday sermon slumber with the mantra on our lips, *Where am I? What happened?* Then, with our new inspiration proven irrelevant, we're left with no other recourse than to push onward along our very personal path of conflicting revelations and confusion.

It may be upsetting, but this path is the only spot in the world where we find real solid ground. This IS reality—at least while playing the game in the physical world. Our personal path is bordered by disillusionment on one side and intimate enlightenment on the other. Step too far one way and there's the abyss of depression. Too far the other way, and we're deluded by glorious descriptions that sweep the emotions far ahead of our actual understanding; in other words, the realm of happy horseshit, which is slippery at best.

Of course, people walk almost everywhere, and we're misled into believing their path is safe. However, as we grow and get heavier, we soon discover where the thin ice is. As the path narrows, as paths always do, the thin ice seems unavoidable. Everywhere we step can look like a mistake. However, in this world of mirrors and mirages, that vision is also an illusion. We get our shoes and socks wet and our feet numbed with cold as the ground we walk on gives way, but it's all part of the program here in this upside down world, where pain is good, and good is always just around the next corner.

We're heirs to the infinite, but we each labor in our own little cubicle, trapped like a genie in a bottle. After we grant a certain number of wishes to a number of masters, will we be given our freedom? Is that what it takes? If not, why are we all bottled up? And what's with all these people telling us what to do?

I suppose I'm here on this planet to do something. I kind of remember a sense of purpose before all the darkness hit, but I really don't remember exactly what I'm supposed to do or why. I believe now that I'm not supposed to know. That's simply not the way the game of fake-out is played. I often imagine beings on the other side of the veil, sitting around laughing as they watch us stumble around in the darkness, bumping into things, getting upset as we learn about light and love from its contrast to the utter darkness.

At this point, it looks to me as if both good and evil are as essential to our earthly path as soul and spirit are to our heavenly one. In fact, they may actually be the natural result our creative mission. I believe the way it has worked is that first God created individual perspectives (souls) as a way to see himself better. Then souls created good and bad to get to know themselves better. If that's true, then both the positive and negative elements in life are actually working for a higher purpose, unseen to us faked-out earthlings.

The other thing I can't help notice is that both seem to be equally wrought with illusions and pitfalls for the unexpecting soul. But then, it looks like that's all part of the game. Both, good and bad, light and dark, all, provide motivation to keep us moving forward creatively and persistently, like a mouse in a maze. Soul reaches down into the difficult and dark, trying to understand how to get to the big cheese. Then it courageously ventures out. We reach up to Spirit for inspiration to push on through the maze, hoping to find fulfillment, a little understanding, maybe a well deserved rest, and eventually, God willing, a place to call home.

To New Thought and Unity
as we journey home

2

<u>Memories of Home</u>

If you've ever watched a flock of birds move in the sky in unison, or a school of fish turn and dart around as if they were one body, you've witnessed firsthand, the divine reality of the One Spirit and the ways of home we've all but forgotten.

We had to set up limits separating ourselves from God in order to play our games and learn our lessons in the earthly world. Still, that was *then*, and this is *now*. And now, as I stand alone on the ground, watching the birds fly together, free, the longing to go home and fly in unison with kindred souls is often overwhelming.

Even when I get out of nature, as if that's ever possible, the reminders of home are all around. Common, high school geometry (like I run into when I occasionally substitute at the local high school) describes pi as an irrational number—as if that really explains anything. Still, they use this "irrational" element to make our world appear rational. You can't measure the area of a circle without using it, but you don't have to look very deep to see that the measurement is just an approximation. We drop the infinite from our description because no one is really interested in the irrational element of this world. Our goal is to make it all make sense, and it does up to a point. However, when we reach that point, Nature has to be recognized for what it is—a profoundly irrational reflection of home.

That isn't to say that it doesn't make sense. It's just that our limited human rational can't quite make sense out of the infinite nature of nature.

Quantum physicists who have bumped up against that irrational wall are noticing that atoms, the building blocks of our "solid" universe, are actually more of a potential than they are something that you can actually always rely on. Bits of matter can simply vanish when you're not looking at them. There's probably someone in another dimension wondering where these little quarks and bosons and electrons came from while we're wondering where they went and why!

Even before quantum physics, back in the 19th century, models relied on accessibility to higher dimensions, to explain where energy and matter went. Today, hundreds of years later, this is becoming a quantifiable study about the energies that flow into and out of our three-dimensional reality.

Our best minds acknowledge that this happens all the time. Little bits of mindless matter are breaking free of our 3D world. It's also been demonstrated that thought can drastically change the crystalline structure of a molecule of water. So, we have matter leaving the world all by itself, and we can observe matter changing by thought alone. If those things aren't reminiscent of how things are back at our original home, I don't know what is!

Then, there are all the physical principles we actually do understand, more or less, which we disguise behind countless, separate scientific laws, simply because the force they all use is applied somewhat differently.

When I was a little boy, I was standing in the shower, playing with the water as little boys do, when I noticed an interesting phenomenon. When two drops fell from two of my fingers, which were close together, the drops always merged into one before they hit the bottom of the shower. Many years later, my son pointed out the same thing with water drops on the windshield.

I know now that this principle that causes water drops to attract each other is called *cohesion*. However, when I was a little boy in the shower wondering about it, the answer I got was that it was because of Love—the same force that causes attraction between people, planets or anything else.

Now, I know the numerous physical principles are all slightly different. However, despite what we know scientifically about all the reasons for all the attractions, the reason I got for the cause behind the cause that day, still makes good sense to me. As far as I'm concerned, it's all most of us (who aren't interstellar rocket surgeons) need to know about the riddle of the unified theory.

It's very clear to the little boy in me that the attraction of love unites schools of fish in their single-minded swim through water and birds in their aerial acrobatics. The idea of flying together in unison, bound by love feels very reminiscent of home. Gaud, I miss it!

Love is probably the best description of God I've ever heard, and it may just be all we need to know about our creator and true home. Imagine that love is a physical law that permeates the ethers. Imagine that it's the natural source from which all other laws result, and that it might just be the cause behind the creation of all animate and inanimate life. Imagine that it's the raw power that fires up the sun and determines its orbit; that it can unite the planets and suns into harmonious interaction and insure the constant creation of life. These are the lessons that are evident in nature and confirmed through contemplation—which leads to stepping out of the limits we all know and the subtle surfacing of memories from home.

Life may not always seem harmonious and loving, but love is what holds all of life together and makes it grow. It's the cause of the ebbs and flows, beginnings and endings of life. The nature of love is full-bodied, round like the sun. So, from where we sit, its light may only be visible part of the time. Still, even when we worry in the shadows, love is always on the rise somewhere.

To New Thought and Unity
away from the darkness

3

The Sun Also Rises

Hemmingway writes about individual survival in what was called "the lost generation," following World War I, in his first and probably most famous novel, *The Sun Also Rises*. The setting is one of moral decay, vanishing illusions, survival, and the destruction of innocence.

Although it pulls at the heart strings to see innocence wiped out, that's probably what growing up is all about. Our bubbles of illusion pop when reality makes its point. I'm afraid that point doesn't seem to change much from one generation to another either. In many ways, we're just as lost today as those that followed WWI, and stories of survival are still just as dramatic.

Learning to survive in the city is obviously much different than learning to survive in the natural wilderness. Also, learning to survive emotionally is different from learning to survive physically, and the skills it takes to survive spiritually are different from anything else! Of course, it can all fit together, but not without a lot of fake-outs along the way.

Everyone has their own story of overcoming the illusion of limits, and the world as a whole has its own story too. Spiritual survival is all about the unifying of all our other skills, attitudes and perspectives. In other words, it's about simplifying everything into a peaceful oneness.

In the beginning, we all had unity consciousness. Since there is only one power in the universe, that's all we knew. However, the attempt to get perspective on this evolved to an attempt to see what else was out there, and we were determined to find something even if we had to create it ourselves. Thus began our strange and conflicting journey into the limits of *Fake-Out Land*.

There's a story about ancient Egypt that seems to parallel this journey. Supposedly, Egypt originally had a religion based on the one God but also on 44 perspectives or aspects of that God. Each perspective was based on the attributes of each of our 44 human chromosomes, since the human body was understood to be holographic of the body of God.

Although humans generally have 46 (23 pairs of) chromosomes now, I'm concluding that the ancient Egyptians only had 44, just like the Aborigines still do today. At any rate, these symbolic representations of our 44 major aspects or attributes came to be known as the neters that were pictured as humans with animal heads—which called attention to particular animal natures in humans. It's said that the ancient Egyptians saw all the aspects of themselves as well as the entire reflective reality of the cosmos in those animal gods.

When Upper Egypt split from Lower Egypt these 44 gods gradually evolved a little independently in each area. Still, all was fine until King Menes reunited the two areas in 3,100 BC All of a sudden, there were 88 gods (44 from both areas combined), and no one could make any sense out of their reflective meaning anymore. Suddenly, the people were very confused, and the illusion of many gods was born.

Akhenaton tried to help his people and straighten all this out by simplifying religion. He tried to streamline things by presenting the all-powerful supreme force as a huge glowing ball of light. It seemed like a perfectly appropriate symbol to use in his attempt to forcefully change his nation's consciousness back in line with unity awareness.

Of course, the people were just fine when they saw his god, which they misunderstood as the sun. However, when they realized that he wanted to trash all the other gods, he had a mutiny on his hands. The people rebelled, just as we rebel against giving up our old habits and illusions.

What you do in a case like that, of course, is kill the messenger. But the concept of unity consciousness was necessary for the world's evolution, so the message of one God rose again. It had always existed in quiet groups here and there—the Hebrews for instance. But the next big painful attempt to push it on the people came with the early Christians.

They created a war zone again by pushing their idea of one God over many gods. All the time, very few, if any, on either side of the battlefield, understood the first thing about peaceful, unity awareness (which is the whole point to the realization of one God). Now, here we are 2000 years later, and it's just beginning to sink in what this one God thing is all about. There are finally some signs of incorporating this religious issue into the reality of our daily perspectives and attitudes. Sure, some of Akhenaton's religion survived. The semblance of a sun disk we see over the Christian saint's heads that we call a halo is probably an example. However, the awareness of one god and our relation to It that grew after Akhenaton died, is his real legacy.

The long, dark night is finally over and the realization of our place in a holographic universe, where big patterns of reality are represented in little things like our chromosomes, is finally dawning again on mankind. We've been faked out for a long time by our own ignorance and by those who yelled the loudest or carried the biggest sticks. Religious rhetoric and authorities have baffled and intimidated us. Their weapons/methods of mass control have only improved over the years. Still, the Sun is also rising. Unity awareness is spreading!

Improved worldwide communication enables people all over the globe to view the same event at just about the same time. Worldwide outcries of injustice are growing. Worldwide empathy and heart felt reactions of support follow all natural disasters these days. People are also becoming aware of unifying into the one heart in these situations.

Tragic events that used to only multiply the suffering, now multiply the love and unity consciousness all over the Earth. When hurricanes or earthquakes claim lives, they immediately trigger this love and unity response, for which we should all be very grateful.

Perhaps, along with our prayers of support for the survivors, we should be sending prayers of thanks for the fallen victims, who gave their lives to help build this heartfelt unity consciousness. With each prayer of love and thanks we send, that huge glowing ball of warm feelings toward all life shines a little brighter and rises a little higher in the sky.

I can see a time when the sun shines brightly high overhead and the lost generations find themselves in a real lasting sort of way. A sense of cooperation for the good of the whole will be in the air, and common concerns will lead to a language every one understands.

That's a pretty likely prophesy for what will happen as humankind matures, because it's exactly what happens when each of us matures. As innocence suffers disillusionment, our self-centered focus becomes aware of a bigger picture. As we consider what may be good for others too, our concerns are tinged with a more enlightened self interest. The benefits of complete cooperation are dawning on us more all the time, but that new world of considering our brother's and sisters needs as equal to our own hasn't quite arrived yet.

We look forward to a time when others will help us realize that goal, and we look back over our lives trying to understand how we might possibly be able to help others get there. Who are we really? What is our unique gift to the world? Is it even possible to know the answers to those questions?

If it is, the answers must lie somewhere in the mix of our past experiences and motivations. What we do and feel paints a pretty good picture of who we are. When placed up against that picture, our thoughts, philosophies and religion are just background noise.

I've retraced my steps my entire life. Even as a kid, I'd wonder about life and about my place in it. I reflected often about how my experiences fit into the grand scheme of things, so those memories have stayed fairly clear. I remember key incidents all the way back to the beginning of my life as if they happened yesterday.

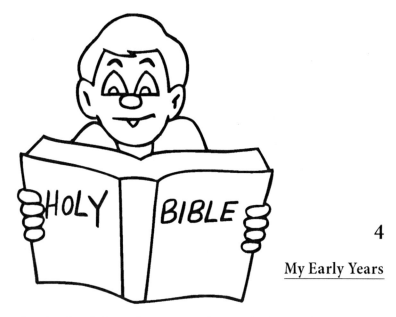

4

My Early Years

After that *head-down, butt-up* incident in the hospital, things were pretty uneventful for a while. I tried to acclimate. I socialized and tried to fit in, but was often conscious of living in another world simultaneously. Channeled information explained these perceptions as the result of memory residue from previous lives that had been encouraged by beings who didn't want me to forget who I am outside of the role I'm currently playing in this world.

My last life explains a lot of the reasons for my current peculiarities. That life culminated into a hermitage in the 1930s and '40s in the jungles of the Yucatan in Mexico. I was told in channeling that I was so psychic back then that I heard everyone's thoughts all the time and had to escape to the mountains to keep from going crazy. There, I talked to the inner guides and animals that would come to me, and was fairly happy living off the land in my little hut, which I kept in meticulous order.

At any rate, as a child in this present life, my instinct was to try to fit into the world better. This urge culminated on the playground when I was in second grade. My friends were playing and I was heading their way from the water fountain while I was simultaneously listening to several guides on the other side. Suddenly, I became very irritated.

"Leave me alone!" I told them, "I just want to be like everyone else!"

While wanting to be like everyone else on their side of the fence is a good thing, here it's an entirely different matter. It took me quite a while to realize what I'd given up in an attempt to fit in better. When that realization finally hit, it was too late. My connection to divine assistance never quite came back the same.

My kids have also struggled with this instinct to try to be like everyone else. One day my son came home from school and didn't want to do his homework because his friends didn't do theirs. We discussed the difference between being shallow, selfish and stupid like his friends, as opposed to fitting in. (I was a little rougher on him than I was later on with his younger sisters.)

It's much harder to fit in without being like everyone else. Yet if we aren't going to explore our own perspective, there's not much reason for being here. The desire to be like everyone else is just one of the universal fake-outs that test our resolve. It stands out as a signpost for many of us as we look back over our lives at what seems to have gone wrong.

After my inner guides backed off, I suppose I appeared fairly normal for a few years. Then, just before I turned ten, all hell broke loose when my father died. It threw me into a passionate search for the truth about life. I literally got religion overnight!

I'd hide under the house and read the Bible. I'd ask questions to the voices in my mind and usually got answers pretty quickly. If the answers didn't come before I went to bed, I'd wake up in the morning with answers. Of course, answers led to more questions, which kept the process going for a while.

At one point, I saw myself as a minister, imparting all the wisdom I was learning. However, after a while, my answers led me past things a minister would normally say. I went to the preacher of my local church to discuss this dilemma. I asked how he handled such situations. He told me that since he was a Methodist minister, he believed what the Methodist seminary taught him.

He had absolutely no appreciation for individuals finding their own answers. My hero and hopes for a glorious career suddenly crashed and burned that day. Soul had successfully sabotaged what looked to me to be my emerging life's mission. I always thought I would have made a great minister! The fact that I suddenly couldn't fit into any orthodox religion that I was aware of was quite a disappointment. Luckily, I didn't know it was to be just one of many dead ends ahead of me, so I took the disappointment in my stride.

I reconciled it by realizing that my answers about life and death were to help me know my own nature, and how I fit into the grand scheme of things. I also was concerned (in a moment of separation from my guidance) that setting myself up as an expert would give me a big head and cut me off from the source of the truth. The idea of capitalizing on my divine guidance also suddenly felt wrong, so I through out all my notes and quotes from the masters.

I was reminded by my guides later (repeatedly) that when I was connected, they would show me my place in life by constantly pointing to how much further there was to go. I could remember how far I've come and look ahead at what there was still to learn. This assured humility even as it reinforced my self confidence.

However, worry about fitting into the world caused me to renew the resolution I had psychically shouted to the heavens on the grammar school playground a few years earlier. I wanted to be left alone to live in this world like everyone else. So, my lessons started coming like they do for everyone else—through the anguish of living life and making mistakes.

I had lots to learn then, just as I do now. I have some regrets—four or five decades of regrets! However, the object of the game in this world isn't to find "Happily Ever After." That's where we started! The point of life, according to Hunt, is to keep an eye on the exit signs that show us the way out of our limitations, but **to live**, get faked-out, and hopefully learn something from the experience.

Illusion holds a very important place in this world. I often wish I could understand everything! Yet, this world wasn't set up that way. The most we can probably expect is to get to know what we need to a little better while we remain blind to all the rest.

*To New Thought and Unity
through innocence to wisdom*

5

Blind is Beautiful

It oftentimes befalls that a father hath a child...devoid of all
perfection, and yet the love that he bears him is such as it casts
a mask over his eyes, which hinders his discerning of the faults
and...makes him rather deem them discretions and beauty...
    –Miguel de Cervantes in "Preface to the Reader"
    regarding his creation of Don Quixote

Although the answers that have unfolded to me have been personally gratifying for the reassurance of order they've presented, I've often wished I could just believe what I was supposed to believe. The more I've learned during my life, the more problems it seemed to cause.

And I set my mind to know wisdom and to know what is
crazy and foolish. I saw that this also is like trying to catch
the wind. Because in much wisdom there is much trouble.
And he who gets much learning gets much sorrow.
    –Ecclesiastes 1:17-18

There you have it! It's in THE book! So here we are, after being plunged into the darkness and limitations of the physical world, trying to make things better, what happens as we succeed? Destruction. Why? Maybe we were meant to operate in darkness until the conclusion / evolution of this 3D world. Or, maybe we have to remove our attention from some things so we can put it more completely on more important things.

Look at what makes an athlete great: Focus—the exclusion of everything possible that doesn't add to the achieving of the goal. A good athlete will often be carefully oblivious to everything except the goal at hand until the athlethic event is is over. So, in that case, and in almost any situation involving goals, more intellect isn't usually better. It's actually an extra burden.

Perhaps spending too much time "learning and verifying things" takes away from a more important focus. Perhaps it detracts from our ability to grasp the magic of life. Perhaps that's the purpose and message that seems to be buried in the history of our planet. If you look at history, every time people accumulated a significant body of knowledge in one place, it was destroyed. The ancient Naacal records are only legendary now. The next greatest loss to the enlightenment of mankind was the Library of Alexandria, which was the object of attacks from 48 BC until 642 AD when it was finally leveled by the Muslims.

The esoteric secrets that were left were almost entirely lost due to the black plague that broke out in China in the early 1300s, and hit Europe in 1347, killing over 25 million people or about a third of the continent. The Catholic Church also systematically mopped up all the remnants of scientific and mystic enlightenment they could find for over 1000 years. From the time Theodosius declared Christianity the sole religion of the Roman Empire in 380 AD, until the inquisitions ended about 1700, all divergent thoughts, many of which were enlightened perspectives trying to poke through to public view, were labeled heresy and dealt with accordingly. Many of these enlightened perspectives were trying to poke through to public view, but they were squelched at every turn.

For instance, the great strides of Galileo and others were stopped in their tracks. Such thinking just wasn't good for business. Combining the Church's objectives for empire with the political empire of the day, they quickly dealt with anyone they could find who didn't tow the party line. Jews and Muslims were their primary targets. However, they also went after any "heretical propositions" they perceived with a vengeance. This included the Lutherans (the first Protestants) and what they called the alumbrados, which translates to "illuminated." This included the practitioners of any mystical or Gnostic forms of Christianity in the 15th and 16th centuries.

Even before the Inquisitions were official, The Church declared war on the Cathers. The Cathers didn't believe in the feudal hierarchy system. They really took to heart what Jesus said about treating the least among us as if they were him, and thus they believed in the equality of all men, including surfs and the poor. Cathers were extremely charitable and peaceful, and they thought the symbol of the crucifix was gruesome and inappropriate, and didn't use it. Also, they were said to possess the "Book of Love,' which was reportedly the teachings of Jesus given to "John the Divine," and accepted as truth by the Knights Templar as well as the Cathers. They resisted the fear the Catholic Church wanted to impose on their religion, and their Gnostic, altruistic beliefs weren't compatible with the mission of the Church. So, of course, they had to be eliminated.

In 1209, the Pope launched a crusade to permanently extinguish their influence. As the story goes, they were so moral and honorable that even some of the soldiers who were sent to butcher them were converted. However, in the end, like everyone else who dared to stand up to the Catholic empire in its formative years, the way of the Cathers was lost to the world.

Today, all examples of peaceful, caring civilizations have been eradicated to the point where we have no living examples of how to create a good, ethical, moral way of life. All those examples were killed off by those who built the foundation for our society today. All we have is our own personal experiences and recognition of what's right in a world where most everything is handled wrong.

Perhaps this is just a case of evil triumphing over good. That's how it's usually presented except by the powers that be. However, like everything else in this world, this evil carnage may not be entirely what it seems.

Look at it this way: First soul left the comfort and light of home for a dark world of illusion and limitations to take a look at what else there was. Then, whenever a significant amount of enlightenment began to accumulate, so this dark world no longer provided a strong contrast to the light and love of home, bam! We had war, suppression, and the lights go out again, so we could continue the original plan of testing and proving souls through the game of fake-out.

It's instinct to try to improve ourselves and the world. That's our job. However, it would appear that, up until now at least, the worldwide foundation of understanding has never really been strong enough to allow the light to shine through too brightly. Walking around in ignorance and blindness was the way our soul chose to: (1) Learn about what God isn't, and (2) grow a heart of compassion, and thus form a natural link back to our original home. So in that sense, blind is beautiful!

I usually feel compassion only after fighting back some pretty strong contempt for the way things are and the people that caused all the darkness. However, since the darkness is a big part of the plan, maybe we should try to be blind to all we've come to know as "good" or "bad."

On a more personal level, I'm not real happy when people give me baloney and tell me it's a steak. However, when I hear positive things that the popular gurus say about humanity and the world, which I know are not actually true, I try not to argue too much with them even in my own mind. What they say they see may not be true right now, but with all the energy they put into that vision, and the belief of their followers, it may be true soon. That's the magic of the "blind is beautiful" principle at its best.

A while ago, I started seeing an email pal's foot (which I never physically saw) as black. My feeling was that something was seriously wrong. I asked, and sure enough there was a long story and a big problem with her foot. Now, as I send her energy and picture it as whole and healed, I don't see it as damaged anymore. I'll stand back at some point and look more objectively, but not right now. That's not the way we cooperate with the "blindness principle" to change things.

Loyalty is blindness. Love is blindness! We dedicate ourselves by choosing what we focus on and to what we wish to remain blind. In this weird world, that's as beautiful as it gets!

Being blind to what is, in favor of what we'd prefer, is a proven way to achieve control over our lives. Without focus, reality is the same, but it's not the same to us. If we look too much at things that have the power to scare us, we tend to get faked out into thinking we were helpless bystanders in our own lives.

Maybe someday, entirely discarding the old dichotomies of truth versus illusion, and good versus bad, will be recognized as a new beautiful blindness that frees us of all our demons of fear, hate and anger. It could be that one day we'll wake up and discover we've forgotten all about the old, archaic polarities.

I was once told of one particular tribe that never discusses what they personally believe with each other. The elders say that such a discussion would only increase the sense of separation among the members of the tribe. Instead, they know what's important. They feel their connection to each other.

Perhaps being blind to all that we believe to be wrong is all we need to move our lives and the entire world forward, out of the dark ages. Maybe that's our choice. Or maybe it can only be the choice of last resort because we're all too beautifully blinded by this fake-out world.

Trying absolutely everything else first would sure drive the lesson home. It always has in my life. I just wonder how long we'll sit up in Heaven, or someplace between here and there, when this life is over, feeling really stupid that we didn't try the answer of detachment and trust—the answer of last resort, a little earlier.

It seems to me that the point that all the world saviors have made, each in their own way, is that using the right answer only after trying absolutely everything else first, probably isn't the wisest thing to do. Every spiritual master I'm aware of has pointed to love and the non-judgmental acceptance of the things as a shortcut out of this limited, fake-out world. It helps blind us to our egocentric view of the world, which makes room for a more enlightened understanding.

> A human being is a part of a whole, called by us universe,
> a part limited in time and space. He experiences himself,
> his thoughts and feelings as something separated from
> the rest ... a kind of optical delusion of his consciousness.
> This delusion is a kind of prison for us, restricting us to our
> personal desires and to affection for a few persons nearest
> to us. Our task must be to free ourselves from this prison
> by widening our circle of compassion to embrace all living
> creatures and the whole of nature in its beauty.
> –Albert Einstein

Trusting the hearts of our brothers and sisters while refusing to insist on our own personal preferences may feel like going out on a limb. However, consider it an investment in getting to know that branch of the family better. Personal priorities are never as important as the heart-warming peace we experience when we widen our *circle of compassion to embrace all living creatures and the whole of nature* in the tree of life.

To New Thought and Unity
of all the branches of life

THE TREE OF LIFE. † THE CHRISTIAN.

6

The Tree of Life

My 12-year-old daughter once introduced me to a wood nymph. The nymph said she liked trees. She said that a few times, and I like trees too, but I just wasn't getting it, so she took me inside one. I was still conscious of being in my physical body, but I was somehow also going with her into the tree. Once inside, I felt much smaller, and was aware of life coursing all around me. I got happier and happier in what seemed like an entire world of its own. The tree was like a lightening rod that brought heaven down to earth, and the world didn't stop at the base of the tree, or even the roots, but was connected to the heart of Mother Earth. The delight of the whole experience was overwhelming, and I still get all quivery when I think about it. I really prefer her world to mine, and I wish I could somehow spend a lot more time there.

Hearing the call of soul after an experience like this, many leave society entirely, as I did in my last lifetime, never to rediscover a place in it. Others, do as I did this time and return to civilized society again and again, and just never really get it right or fit in very well. We each do what we can to behave reasonably and still honor that unique truth inside. Yet, there's unmanifested potential inside that seed, just waiting for any opportunity to express itself. It's a tree we don't own, but which actually owns us. Given what it needs, that little sprout can really assert itself, letting us know who's in charge in no uncertain terms. Once sprouted, the growth and demands of one's soul can uproot many a peaceful and orderly life and cause us to make decisions that may not seem reasonable to anyone else.

The goal, of course, is to incorporate the depth and needs of soul into a life full of interaction with others. This also spreads the awareness of soul consciousness as we quietly walk through our days. However, this new, higher order doesn't come as easily or as simply as the desire for change. Not fitting into society, along with some remnants of precious memories of totally belonging in our true home, has caused many of us some serious anguish. However, anguish appears to be the food a soul seeks in this world.

Sometimes a peak enlightening experience, or a surprise awareness of the love of others can shock us out of our egocentric lives, and bless our roots with a little more growth. Other times, discipline, and well placed attention is all it takes to keep things growing in the right direction.

> When we become spiritualized by self-discipline and deep
> meditation, we soar like the wind in the omnipresence of our
> true soul nature.
> –Paramahansa Yoganada

However, I really believe the method most used to achieve the most dramatic realizations of getting in touch with soul is pure and simple suffering. Fortunately, most lives provide ample opportunity to get shocked out of a comfort zone and into some deeper realization. It may be a serious illness, a near death experience, a death of a loved one, a divorce, (or living in need of one), or some other traumatic experience.

If you're going through this, count your blessings! The real tragedy would be when a person can't separate enough from daily priorities to do his/her soul work until they're on their death bed. I think I'd rather never get that perspective than to get it when it's too late to really do anything about it.

I used to belong to an organization that advocated, as Saint Francis put it, "dying daily." This is a regular discipline of withdrawing from the world and getting in touch with who we really are. After fourteen years of study, I was initiated as a "brother of the leaf." This came with a sense of belonging and purpose. I was just one of many brothers on a tree with many leaves. Today, I'm here to tell you, there are many, MANY trees in the forest of Divine Spirit.

The way of soul is to sink roots down into the darkness, searching out nutrition while we branch out looking for light and love. Although the process is the same for everyone, everyone experiences it and grows differently from that experience. Each seed is a unique creation with a unique, unlimited potential and a unique path.

On the other hand, those who choose not to answer the call of soul in this lifetime can usually find a quick and respectable place among the rest of the shallow rooted. Honorable authorities in schools and churches preach fear and fragmented truths to keep the roots of their followers boxed up for easy transplanting. Corporations also cooperate by giving these folks jobs, and appreciating them greatly because they're so predictable and controllable. Those air-conditioned, florescent-lit cubicles aren't nearly as comfortable or necessary as they might seem sometimes, but that's always an option.

Many soul driven people will find places in corporations, but only after they've shaken all the muddy social obligations from their roots. Our little boxes suddenly fall off once Soul takes its rightful place as the authority over our lives. We're suddenly free to take heart and take root!

*To New Thought and Unity
with our inner authority*

7

Lessons from the Authorities

After high school, I really didn't know what I wanted to do, so I moved out and took a little time off. When I finally started college I took mostly fun courses like Philosophy, Psychology, Sociology, Art Appreciation, and stuff like that. The first two years went great! Even while working to pay my expenses, I still got mostly As.

Then, my parents had a talk with me to discuss my future. I'd been thinking that teaching at the college level was a good goal. They said that was a dead end job. They said I'd probably never make any real money. They said I should switch to a business major, and if worse came to worst, I could still teach. However, a business major would open up other possibilities for me.

That sounded reasonable. It wasn't what I wanted to do, but what did I know? I was just a dumb kid, and they were older and wiser. There were two of them, only one of me, and they were my parents. So, I switched my major, and immediately began having trouble with the business and technical courses. I hated every minute of it, and did really poorly.

Anyone who wanted to hire a business graduate wanted an MBA. So my options were severely limited until I got more experience or more education, which I couldn't even consider at the time. The only jobs I qualified for with my BS in Business Administration were the ones that didn't care what I majored in.

I thought that I had ruined my life forever, but that also proved to be just another fake-out. Eventually, channeled information revealed that taking my parent's advice was part of my prelife contract, and it sent me in the direction I was supposed to go. I was young and weak, and it was planned that I'd defer to their judgment.

However, that was also the first of many experiences that made me start to realize the value of my own insights as opposed to trusting anyone else with my life. There's a line from the movie *Young Einstein*, which asks, "If you can't trust the governments of the world, who can you trust?"

I think we all know the answer to that question. We have to trust our establishments to some degree. Yet, without going into bitter sounding particulars about any or all of our fine institutions, the less trust we turn over to them or anyone the better!

Sooner or later, we all have to learn to trust our own insights and take as much responsibility for our lives as possible. This can be hard sometimes. However, confidence in ourselves builds when we finally realize the value of the alternative.

It would be nice to get a little good advice now and then. Still, sometimes it feels like authorities keep intruding in our lives simply to reinforce the lessons of our general earthly fake-out.

Authorities and Life in general, both teach us:
1. To trust ourselves by first trusting others;
2. What's right by doing what's not; and
3. What we love by suffering what we don't.

Trusting authorities over our own instincts with our personal lives is just another way to help drive those life lessons home. Those who need more reinforcement of those lessons might well want to keep deferring to others, because in this weird world of fake-outs, that's how we learn!

However, at some point, suffering somehow begins to lose its appeal. That's when it's time to climb out of the old familiar nest feathered with advice, and take the leap of faith. Trust that the wings of self reliance can carry you at least through the clouds of confusion to where angels wait. Then, as you might imagine, learning to fly with their help holds the key to the expression of each little bird's uniqueness.

8

Inner Guidance

I think that one of the definitions of being certifiably "out-of-it" is hearing voices that no one else can hear. So, I'm not saying that I hear voices, exactly, but I do get messages. That still probably separates me from the ranks of the recognizably rational, but I guess I'll still come out of the closet and admit that I've gotten these messages my whole life.

Yet, that never has really made me immune to the illusion of limits in this fake-out world. Whenever I've asked Spirit what I'm supposed to do, the answer I've almost always gotten has been: *What do you want to do?*

I keep asking because I keep thinking that there's got to be someone, somewhere who knows more than I do about what's going on! This is a lot like looking for a physical authority to make our choices easier, except that inner guidance usually isn't as specific as guy's drinking buddy or a girl's best friend might be:

Do whatever you want to do.

I got that a lot. In retrospect, I can see that's pretty good advice, but at the time it's like not getting any advice at all. When I push it, I'll also get cautions, perspectives, possible ramifications, but when it comes to making choices, usually there's only silence.

Yet, if I ask specific questions, I'll often get specific answers. For illustration purposes, I'm going to give you a quick synopsis of the answers

I've gotten that pertain to one of my favorite subjects, and one I think may be near and dear to the hearts of many: romance.

I greatly respect anyone who can make a relationship work "for better or worse...until death do you part." However, over half of the marriages today end up in divorce. I hope that relating my story of inner guidance, starting before I entered this world where two marriages were prearranged, might give those people some comfort.

I'm coming out of the closet and going out on a limb here by telling a very personal story that is probably going to be very difficult for many to believe. I just hope you can reserve judgment long enough to catch a sense of order in life that I think this story reflects. I also hope many might gain an appreciation for the potential of their own inner guidance. That awareness and appreciation can literally open up whole new worlds to you! End of preamble.

Story time: Once, a long, long time ago, before I married ex #2, I asked Spirit if someone who would be a better match for me might be coming along. The answer I got was unbelievably specific:

She'll have dark hair, like to give massages, be a good cook... Everything this guide said hit my hot buttons. I was told she would also be a member of the little spiritual organization to which I belonged, sort of a requirement at the time. In short, she was absolutely perfect for me! She was so perfect, that when the contemplation was over, after a moment of reflection, I said out loud, "Yeah, right!"

The vision was of such a seemingly perfect partner, and it seemed like such a long shot to me, that I simply couldn't believe it. I married the woman I was dating, so I could get on with my goal of having a family, and forgot all about this inner experience, until one day about a year later.

A new face appeared in our little group. She had just moved here, and I recognized her immediately as the woman from my vision a year earlier. I was already married, so I couldn't do anything about it. Several months later, she moved out of town. She told us she wasn't even sure why she moved to our community in the first place.

For the next decade or so, whenever I thought of her, I saw intimate details of an alternate life with her. I didn't even believe in alternate lifetimes at the time! I had read about them, and my logical mind had decided that's not how life works. Still, whenever I thought of her, I was surprised by the developments in our lives together since the last time I'd checked in. What I didn't realize until much later was that the life I was seeing was coming through so strongly because it was my contracted life, and by marrying someone else I was actually living the alternative life.

At any rate, I saw when a dark haired baby girl was born into our lives. I saw her grow up. I saw the marital trouble we had, and then I saw us separate. I looked on as we got back together, and I felt our sadder but more loving resolution. I saw past lives we had together, and how karma was being worked out.

I was constantly haunted for well over a decade by the nightmare of my mistake of marrying before meeting her. I saw visions for about 18 years, but after I saw us get divorced, I stopped watching for a while. Then, I saw the man I was in that alternative lifetime die—right on schedule as specified by my pre-life contract. It may be hard to imagine that a life where I died was the planned path but that's another story (covered in my book *Looking, Seeing & Knowing*).

Another indication that marriage #2 was actually a mistake came on my honeymoon. As soon as we arrived at the little motel, I put my bag on the bed and a guide, who had evidently just returned, shouted, "Oh no!"

He said, "Go home! Get it annulled!"

I think sometimes people think of guides as little Gods, but many of them aren't even full time guides. Sometimes, they're just concerned souls who drop by now and then. In this case, this was a member of my soul family who suddenly felt responsible for getting my life back on track, and he overreacted a little.

I listened to him and felt the importance of his guidance, but I thought I could always get a divorce. I had a nice weekend planned. I figured that since I was already married, I should just wait now and see how things go. I didn't see any reason to act radically.

He threw up his hands, and left. I had a nice weekend. Then, eleven years later the desire for a divorce was mutual.

The guidance that weekend made me start wondering how much we're supposed to trust someone's advice over what we think we want to do (even if they may have a better perspective). I felt that I made a big mistake for many years by not following the guidance to get that marriage annulled. However, I made a statement that day about taking responsibility for my life, and that's been a foundation on which my inner guidance has helped me build, one precariously placed stick and stone at a time ever since.

After marriage #2 finally resolved, I quickly found someone else to marry. However, it wasn't too long before I started wondering what would have happened if I hadn't married her. My old hermit instincts were kicking in, and I was thinking about moving to Montana. So, I wondered what would have happened if I had moved there instead.

That's all it took. Instantly, I saw a woman living in the hills who was very psychic and seemed to be waiting for me. When the marriage started to go bad a year or so later, I checked in again. She was still waiting. Several years later, the same thing happened. I started to wonder what was going on. I could feel her situation changing, but every time I checked in psychically, I confirmed that she was still waiting for me. As I eventually looked closer, I got the message that she was almost ready for me, and I continued to get that message for years!

After I moved to Montana with wife number three and after she told me one of us had to move out, I met a woman online who lived in the hills and proved to be very psychic. Being around her was like opening a door to another world. Spirits would talk to me more easily than I'd ever experienced.

Still, when I first talked to her on the phone, I found myself saying, "You're not the one." I don't know where that came from, or why I said it out loud. Even more interesting though was that I felt compelled to fight the flow and try for several years, on and off, to make her "the one."

During that time, I asked what would have happened if I never married ex #3. I saw myself moving to Missoula and commuting on the motorcycle I always wanted to Hamilton to see her. It was a very loving but difficult relationship, and that's all I got for quite a while. However, I saw how it ended after some other stories came together opening me up to that realization.

In my real life, I did occasionally date her and always wished it could be more. However, when ever I thought of the full time loving companion I wanted, I'd get the message; "After all you've gone through, imagine how'd you feel if she died right after you felt settled." Sometimes it was posed as a question, but that was the gist of the message I got repeatedly for several years.

I usually thought that was just fear talking. However, remember I said I was supposed to die earlier according to my precontracted life? Well, even though I took a different fork in the road, I was still scheduled to check out during that phase of my life. So, here's the rest of the story:

If I never married ex #3, I would have moved to Missoula and seriously dated or maybe married, let's call her, Tonya (even after knowing that she was not "the one.") We would have had a bumpy, but intensely loving relationship. Then, she would have succumbed to cancer. That was part of her contract. Since I never had the kids from ex #3 to anchor me, I would probably also have fulfilled my contract by taking my own life.

That's just a possibility, but it's one I could easily see play out because the inclinations to fulfill my contract were hardwired into my relationship with this life. The universe continued to lead me to a place where I could check out without any regrets, per my contract, regardless of my personal choices along the way. When I entered that final phase of my precontracted life, I had a certain mental predisposition.

However, on the path I physically took, I had kids and didn't move to Missoula. I still got to know Tonya after my divorce, and after trying for a while to get closer, I had a dream that our house blew up. That morning, she pulled out her tarot cards and immediately drew a card that had almost the exact same imagery. We decided to not see each other after that, but we corresponded regularly for about five years. Then, she passed away right on schedule.

It felt tragic! Yet seeing the alternative life with her where she died, and having that caution from my guides in this life not to move in together because she might be moving out of this world, feels like confirmation that her tragic death was preordained, and she probably planned it just like I know (from channeled information) that I planned mine.

During the time I corresponded with her I found two other women I thought I might want to marry. Neither of those very short relationships worked out either.

My guides tried to warn me about one of them. Of course, I argued. Then, to illustrate his point, one of them showed me a television full of static. I explained that under all that static I believed she was probably a good person and that love could probably bring that out.

Another guide came along and was also very concerned that I was pursuing the relationship. He was struggling with what to say when the first guide showed him the TV with all the static he had showed me.

This second guide then said, "Yes! That's it exactly! See?"

Anyway, I left them shaking their heads. Needless to say, there was horrible static in that relationship and it ended with me wishing I had just listened to my guides.

I never said to anyone, "You're the one," until I met the third serious prospect. She was everything I had asked for and envisioned. When I'd put out my requests for what I wanted in a partner, I'd hear, "We're working on it." I heard that over and over whenever I told the guides something else I'd like.

After I found myself saying, "You're the one," to #3; after I'd effused my most powerful prayers of thanks for weeks, I discovered I was faked-out again. After loaning/giving her a bunch of money when I thought we were engaged, she told me she simply couldn't leave her area, which was out of state. She had said at the beginning that moving wasn't a problem, but when it became one, our relationship was suddenly and coldly concluded.

However, it turns out she was "the one." Like every significant event in my life up to that point, it didn't turn out the way I'd hoped and expected, but I'd always gotten what I needed. I was picturing a blissful home life with an ever-present, loving partner who would put an end to the empty spot I had inside. It seems that my higher self saw fit to deliver a woman who would put an end to my suffering but without all that other stuff, which had to do with a permanent relationship.

After that very short romance broke up, something clicked inside. It could have pushed me into fulfilling my contract and leaving this world, but instead I went the other way. I gave up on finding a woman to complete me, and decided I was happier and better off alone. I also began to feel a more loving connection to the life I already had, and a stronger connection to the guides around me.

It also occurred to me right after that experience, that all of life was a minefield of fake-outs, many fake-outs all leading to one big fake-out if we aren't careful, and I started writing this book.

That's when my life started all over. It seems there was another psychic woman in the hills of Montana. Billy confirmed that my original vision about a woman waiting for me was really about her. Also, her guides led her to believe that if she moved to Montana, she'd find me. When she had a dream about living in Montana and being "extremely happy," she just picked up and moved, and waited, and waited....

I had gotten guidance to move to Montana about the same time. So in 1996, we both moved here. However, I was still married for another four years, and we didn't meet until six years after my divorce. So, after Danna moved to Montana, she had to wait ten years to meet me!

During that time, whenever I asked my guides about the woman in my vision who was waiting for me, I was told, "she's not quite ready" to meet me yet. I was told this for almost ten years! As it turns out, she wasn't ready to meet me because as far as any of her guides knew, there was a good chance I could fulfill my contract and leave this world at any time.

We both read the same personals ads for five years without finding each other. Then, after that little incident with the woman who was "the one," (Is that twisted guidance or what?) I finally became reliable enough to be allowed to meet Danna.

She channeled an entity who told me he led us together, and congratulated us on following the clues. Maybe that was one of his main jobs, because after we both were sold on each other, he stopped coming through, and Danna started channeling her brother, Billy. Billy has provided a safety net for many of my thoughts ever since. I can confirm experiences and perspectives with him, and he fills in the details when I ask.

So, I've suddenly been doubly blessed: by Danna who has been a rock in the tumultuous sea of my life; and by the entities she channels, who help me keep life in perspective and give me challenges to improve myself, one issue, and one clue at a time.

Now, for the first time since taking that fork in the road (when I married ex #2) away from my precontracted plan, I finally feel my life taking on a new constructive order. I've learned a new appreciation for my own inner guidance and a new awareness of myself. I continue to follow clues along a meandering path, and I can see how all the little pieces of my life are beginning to fall into place. Once in a while, I even get glimpses of bigger picture.

I'm constantly reminding myself these days that in Fakeoutland, mirages are a lot more common that reality. I'm always trying to see past the illusion and beneath the surface of things. This sends out an invitation to the guides for help with that picture.

The questions they carefully answer usually only raise more questions. Still, that process has gotten me in touch with the reality of life and my power over my apparent limitations like never before. Love is finally in the forefront of my awareness. I feel it more every day from my family and from the inner guides who are always at work behind the scenes to help keep us on track.

Since the lessons have been a blessing, the suffering that brought on those lessons must also have been a blessing. So, life is just one big adventure of love and lessons. We may have other plans, but it's what happens on our way to our goals and out attitude about it that really makes up a soul enriching life.

It's been my experience that whatever the lesson, it eventually brings us around to a deeper awareness of the love that surrounds us on every possible plane. Knowing this brings the security of peace and happiness no matter what's going on in our lives. And a person who learns to be happy no matter what's going on in their life has learned the secret to limitless joy.

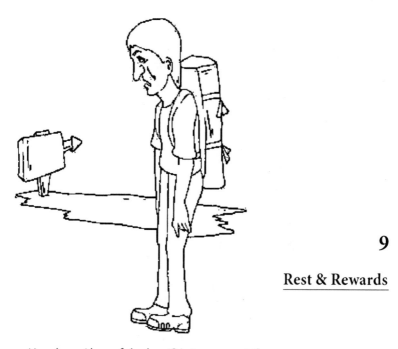

How have I been faked-out? Let me count the ways.
I've been faked-out to the depth and breath of my being.
I've been faked-out by touch, sound and seeing;
Faked-out as I strive for what's right
Even as I struggle with all of my might.
My heart and soul long for the love of home.
Still, stumbling through Fakeoutland I roam.

It just so happened that while the realization of one of my romantic fake-outs was dawning on me, a *Star Wars* movie was coming out. It was a stormy realization that hit me with all the thunder and lightning of dreams shattering and hopes flying apart. I had gotten really attached to the idea of finally doing the marriage thing right.

Yoda had advice in that movie that reminded me of the old lesson I was hoping would just go away. Here is an excerpt from a movie review I sent the woman whom I thought was "the one."

> *I think attachment to people and things and fear of losing*
> *them just makes us weak and vulnerable. The way of the*
> *Jedi is one of love and service, with a mystic relationship to*

*the force. The way of the dark side is one of selfishly trying
to control things without regard to cooperation with the
will of the universe. This probably happens because of a fear
that cooperative service to the loving nature of the universe
won't get us what we want. It seems to me that the moral of
the story is that forcibly taking things into our own hands to
get what we think we need or deserve, or are afraid we won't
get otherwise, can only end in regrets and a lesson that
brings us back to the middle path—the one of trust, service,
and detachment.*

Jessie later corrected this statement in the light of the polarization that is currently going on in this world. It seems the path of control (the dark side) may have the option of an interesting detour coming up in the near future so that people's expectations (rewards) can be realized in a deeper way than ever before. This shift will also provide everyone with a restful timeout from the tension caused by the conflict between the "service to others" and the "service to self" factions. But that's another story (covered in *Looking, Seeing & Knowing*, by yours truly).

Getting back to my movie review and personal comments, I continued:

*I have to trust that when the universe knows it's time for
my rest or reward, that I'll find a peaceful, loving spot for a
while. It would be such a blessing if that loving spot never
turned out to be anything other than what it appears at
face value. However, if it turns out to be just another lesson
in detachment, then I'll keep learning and growing until I'm
really ready, and the rest from surprises finally presents itself.*

I wasn't quite so positive when writing in my journal. I rambled on, chronicling related events on my mind as some sort of explanation just in case something happened to me:

*Over the years, as I've asked why things turned out the way
they did, I saw my errors, character flaws and weaknesses. I*

saw sins from past lives, and I learned about the karma that never dies by itself.

Proceeding through life with very little trust and almost no patience has led me to make bad marriage decisions, so that when my contracted love came along, I was in no position to do anything about it. Still, when I think of her, I remember several beautiful past lives together. I also remembered a past life where my wife was brutally taken from me. So between anger, disappointment and self- pity, I'm a real mess!.

I had hope for a better day, and I even have some pretty solid reassurances from my spiritual guides. Still, the glorious premonitions are losing their power to impress me as my promised pot of gold keeps retreating further with every new rainbow. They've only led to endless lessons, and the vision of peace, love, and a powerful intimacy with a kindred soul has always been an illusive dream.

Maybe detachment will eventually enlighten me to some sort of realization of joy in this world. But I'm just not sure I'm going to make it that far. Without a loving, intimate relationship, I don't really even want to try anymore. I want love or out—more every day.

Years later, after I met Danna, it was confirmed through channeling that the romance I missed was, in fact, arranged before coming into this world. It was also confirmed that my growing tendency to pull the plug on my physical life was also a cooperative instinct with my prelife contract. However, missing the contracted romance set things up so my planned departure from this world was also more tentative. On the other path I died of an aneurism. On this path, I took better care of my body and started to make a plan for a longer life, so the check-out clause was suspended. Only the residue of wanting to leave the world remained, and life's disappointments brought it out for quite a while.

We all have to cooperate with the universe whether we like it or not and whether we understand it or not. As it turned out, that period of my life was the darkest spot before the dawn. I was learning to be okay without a close companion. Then, after my attitude shifted and I changed my fate, the companion who had been waiting suddenly came out of the mist to help me heal and begin again.

I've received crash courses on the lessons of life for as long as I can remember. First, I'll crash, and THEN I'll learn the lessons.

Disappointments can be pretty intense sometimes, but it's never worked for me to make desperate demands of God. Our effects on the world are profound, and our control over our own lives is absolute, but not in the way we normally think about "control." Our effect on the world around us is a mystical one, and it seems to be unaffected by all but the lightest touch.

Since, learning detachment from outcomes may be a big part of our lesson in this world; we just may find that we NEVER get what we think we want. Still, we can grow in compassion and understanding no matter what happens, and that just may be the point of being here in the first place. Then, when we don't really care what happens, things do change. When we no longer need them to, they do change. This isn't the way I'd design life if anyone ever asked me, but I think it's the way it works.

It's all a blessing—all the twists of fate that often bring about the thing we fear the most. This whole system of fake-outs seems to be part of a bizarre plan to bring us blessings that aren't related to any personal goal. When the fake-outs have run their course, and we can finally surrender our agendas to that unseen intelligence behind all things, the skies suddenly look a lot bluer.

10

Blue Skies

Awhile back, during a depressing, wintry period, while taking my daily stroll "down the valley of the shadow of death," I suddenly found myself humming a little tune. Then, to my surprise, I actually started singing: "Blue skies, coming my way, nothing but blue skies all day." I couldn't get it out of my head for weeks!

The only thing I can think of to explain it is that I must have been touched by an angel. It probably tried many times to plant a positive thought. I probably just said, "Nah, no way!" But this happy little song snuck into my consciousness and pried open my mind and I found myself thinking, "Maybe…"

That silly little tune and the thought of the happy irony of blue skies in the middle of all my darkness, was enough to snap me out of the depression. I started looking at nature as comforting, and the elements in it as family. In time, blue skies and trees and all of nature became my lifeline.

I think it's interesting that the word nature comes from the Latin word, *natus*, which means "to be born."

That sort of says it! The word itself seems to imply that until we're reborn to the realization of our unity with the natural, wild world, we just aren't quite alive yet. Nature is enchanting, magical and enduring— just like soul. Learning to be alive as soul, is all about our personal vision and interaction with the infinitely deep and varied life of nature. To feel vulnerable, fragile, or afraid we might not get our share of the limited resources, is to choose the world of man at the expense of our awareness of the abundance of nature. True, some things are limited, but the creativity of soul can handle that! It can turn any bad experience into a good one in time if that's what needs to be done. In the meantime, this connection to the natural world tunes us into our own joyful nature.

In the world of fake-outs, we have to be willing to take chances and trust our indestructible nature. It seems to me that in this upside down world, the safest road can often lead to the most serious disappointments, like when I changed my college major to "cover my bases." Since then, I've come to believe that we shouldn't be faked-out by what we think is safe or normal, when what's natural is so much better!

When we live with passion, letting our heart lead us as if no one can hurt us and no mistakes are possible, suddenly the skies clear and life is worth living again. When we stop feeling the failure from past fake-outs and focus instead on the constant blue of the sky, suddenly everything makes sense. The sun is always shining up there somewhere. So, blue skies are always coming our way—no matter what happens.

11

Hunt's Law

I started out my morning with another little mistake, which I don't even want to talk about. It did inspire this conclusion though: "Anything that can fake us out will!"

Sound familiar? A man named Murphy has been accredited with coming up with something very similar back in 1949. Capt. Edward A. Murphy was an Air Force engineer in charge of a project designed to see how much sudden deceleration a person can stand in a crash. One day, when something went wrong with the wiring, exasperated with a technician, he yelled, *"If there is any way to do it wrong, he'll find it!"*

The guy who was supposed to ride that deceleration sled, pulling 40 Gs, Dr. John Paul Strapp, wrote it down, generalizing it into, "Whatever can go wrong, will," and called it Murphy's Law. Then, he presumably sighed in relief that he wouldn't be taking that sled ride for a while and went on a coffee break.

The experiment was eventually completed, and in a PR statement to the press, Strapp said that their success was due to everyone's efforts to circumvent Murphy's Law. However, I think what he wrote down after the experiment is much more interesting. In what became known as "Strapp's Ironical Paradox," he states, "The universal aptitude for ineptitude makes any human accomplishment an incredible miracle."

Amen, Brother!

❧ ❧

Why don't things go the way they're expected? Why do surprises ruin all our best plans? Why are occurrences that save us from all these crazy disappointments so miraculous? It's simply because we fell down the rabbit hole, and landed in Fakeoutland! The chances here of doing a thing wrong are infinitely higher than doing it right. That makes doing anything right on one of your first tries, downright miraculous.

Besides that, I firmly believe that things were set up in this world to purposefully deceive us. I don't mean that in an overly pessimistic or bitter way. I'm simply making an observation and wondering about the cosmic plan behind it all. Maybe, it's all part of a lesson designed to take our attention off the things that almost never go right, and put it on the constancy of the blue skies and our limitless potential.

Potentially, we can all be patient, trusting, graceful, and charitable. I tend to think that's the way things should be. However, on this side of the fence, what comes naturally is anxiety over our immediate personal concerns. Challenges continually test us to see if we're going to "sink or swim." So the subtleties of attitude like patience and gracefulness often get lost in the struggle if we aren't constantly mindful of them.

The waters churn; the undertow and currents keep surprising us! Acting with trust and charity sometimes seems like unfair tests at those times. Yet that's when we're tested, and "sinking" into a lower state of existence isn't the only alternative.

We'll more than likely get a mouthful or two as the waves of the fake-out world relentlessly wash over us. Things will probably go wrong in ways we can't even imagine right now. Still, considering our infinite timetable, I expect we're all destined to become great swimmers in the karmic ocean of life! The trick is to not get in over our heads whenever we can avoid it.

12

The Fairer Sex

T alking about getting in over our heads, it's a cheap shot, but I have to take it: There's nothing fair about the fairer sex! Maybe there used to be. Or maybe it's just one of those sarcastic misnomers like calling a really big man "Tiny."

Women may look and sound soft, but if ever there were a good example of undertows and surprising currents in the great ocean of life, relations with the opposite sex would be it! I know women have trouble with shallow guys, but my experience is mostly with the trouble us, simple minded, unsuspecting, guys have with women. This is just the opinion of someone who's been divorced three times, but it seems to me that as misleading as this world is, generally, relations with the opposite sex multiplies those odds against us.

Socrates said, *"If you marry well, you'll be happy. If you marry poorly, you'll be a philosopher."*

I've done both now. However, I have to admit that the philosopher in me is still alive and well. As the story goes, Socrates married the meanest hag in town in order to prove to his followers that one can be peaceful and happy no matter what the circumstances. However, as a third grader once put it, "He died from an overdose of matrimony."

I have a lot of philosophies on women, but I don't trust my objectivity anymore. So, I walked through the hall of records (surfed the net) to see what others had to say on the subject.

Women who are inclined to be insulted might want to just skip ahead to the next topic, although, they may not find the subject of lunacy that much more to their liking. I'm sure a case could be made against men as a whole too, but then that's what history is all about.

For what it's worth, here's a sampling of what others have said about the mysterious and probably most famous fake-out of them all, relations with the fairer sex:

> *Woman is a miracle of divine contradictions.*
> –Jules Michelet

That's almost flattering.

> *Is not marriage an open question, when…such as are in the institution wish to get out, and such as are out wish to get in?*
> –Ralph Waldo Emerson

Excellent observation, Ralph. Here's the same thing said a little differently:

> *The poor wish to be rich, the rich wish to be happy, the single wish to be married, and the married wish to be dead.*
> –Ann Landers

> *I've had bad luck with both my wives. The first one left me and the second one didn't.*
> –Patrick Murray

Warming up to the "lowest common denominator" sort of comments, here are some opinions by H.L. Mencken:

> *Love is the delusion that one woman differs from another.*

> *Bachelors know more about women than married men; if they didn't they'd be married too.*

*I never knew what real happiness was until I got married,
and by then it was too late.*

From Oscar Wilde, we have: "Dammit sir, it's your duty to get married. You can't be always living for pleasure."

Marriage is not a word; it is a sentence.
–King Vidor

*Ah, yes, "divorce," From the Latin for "having your genitals
torn off through your wallet."*
–Robin Williams

*Getting married the second time is a triumph of hope over
experience*
–Unknown

*When I have one foot in the grave, I will tell the whole truth
about women. I shall tell it, jump into my coffin, pull the lid
over me and say, "Do what you like now."*
–Leo Tolstoy

*God made men big and strong so we wouldn't have to be
afraid of women; it didn't work.*
–PC Seldom

*Heaven hath no rage like a love to hatred turned, Nor hell a
fury like a woman scorned.*
–William Congreve

Love is temporary insanity curable by marriage.
–Ambrose Bierce

*In marriage, there are three rings; the engagement ring, the
wedding ring, and the suffering.*
–Unknown

Now…to end this on a more constructive note:

*Love is an ideal thing, marriage a real thing; a confusion of
the real with the ideal never goes unpunished.*
–Goethe

"Confusion of the real with the ideal never goes unpunished." A better description of the divine comedy of human existence I've never heard. Like many of the kids who grew up during the *Ozzi and Harriet/Father Knows Best* era, I glowed with romantic expectations about the future. Then life happened.

Like life, many of the quotes above just aren't very funny if you think about them too much. But then that's the choice. We can either laugh at things (and relationships) that we can't understand and keep moving, or we can think too much and go crazy.

13

How Crazy Are We?

*The statistics on sanity are that one out of every 4 Americans
are suffering from some form of mental illness. Think of your
three best friends. If they're okay, then it's you.*

—Rita Mae Brown

Following the demands of our heart and soul can lead to some maddening experiences. However, if we don't follow our heart, we're probably going to go crazy anyway in what becomes for many of us, a very mundane, exhausting, unsatisfying world. As this dissatisfaction grows, we have to do something new and maybe drastic, to change things!

One must do mad things when he loves madly.
—Ben Franklin

However, the disruption of making changes can also drive us crazy, and if we make overly drastic changes... Well, it's hard to even appear balanced when life gets really desperate. In other words, for various reasons, whether we're going crazy because we need change in our lives or because we're in the middle of one, many of us are generally at least a little off the edge most of the time.

～～

It all started back with the original plunge. We jumped off the edge of paradise to learn about love basically from pain and suffering. That's a lot like asking to be beat up so you'll know how good it feels when it's over. You have to admit, we've got to be a little crazy to do that!

However, attributing the original plunge to some sort of original mistake on our part just adds a debilitating craziness to the necessary and adventurous variety. Taking the plunge was a choice. Those who carry that decision as an eternal evil around our neck never push the creative boundaries that are necessary to give souls full expression in this world. In fact, those who are chained to that immobilizing institutional dogma of sinful origins simply don't have any choice but to be saddled with what looks like a very sane sadness.

The rest of us feel compelled to do crazy things to make the original plunge worthwhile. Sure our path will cross some lines, or maybe we'll walk them like a tightrope. It's all a balancing act and a matter of occasionally trying to push those limits around so we don't have to cross them. Relatively normal people are making choices now that would make our ancestors label us as lunatics: Gay marriages, bungee jumping, full grown adults running—for fun.

Perhaps people expect more out of life now. Or maybe life itself has just gotten more dynamic. Either way, life is dynamic enough these days to keep most of us at least a little off balance most of the time. So personally, I'd never presume to sit in judgment about where the lines should be drawn.

Oscar Levant said basically the same thing: "There's a fine line between genius and insanity. I have erased this line."

Drawing lines between good and bad, sane and insane in this crazy world has got to be a little arbitrary. Still, I can't help wondering how crazy all of us (some more than others) are exactly.

My third ex, whom one of my friends calls, "reality challenged," was explaining to me before we were married about her issues and therapy, and it sounded like she was warning me. So I finally asked, "How functional exactly are you?"

She had a very clever response, which made me think her brain worked. However, what I later found out was that a functioning wit does not a functioning person make. She also told me how most of her family had emotional disorders. I thought it had somehow skipped her, but I'd been faked-out again!

I had that influence on one side and my kids on the other, and anyone who's ever had kids knows what that can do to a person.

> *Insanity is hereditary—you get it from your children.*
> –Sam Levenson (*Diners Club Magazine,* Nov 1963)

On the other hand, maybe by comparison to the world in which we live, we're all in great shape!

Think about it:

> *Insanity in individuals is something rare—but in groups,*
> *parties, nations, and epochs it is the rule.*
> –Friedrich Nietzsche

Countries preach the standard for civilized behavior, yet they literally get away with murder. We may employ rationalization occasionally to justify our actions, but they have full-time crews to spin their propaganda.

Relations between the sexes, national and international affairs.... There are so many really great examples of conflicts and fake-outs! I wonder what that makes us for going along with it all and trying to stay positive—crazy?

One of history's most legendary lunatics doesn't think so:

> *To see the world as it is instead of the way it should be is the*
> *craziest thing of all!*
> –Don Quixote

*To New Thought and Unity
with divine inner peace*

14

Magic Mantras

As I walked at dawn down the magnificently manicured path on the Sho-hondo Temple grounds in Japan, the sounds of chanting morning gongyo coming from the humble homes on each side resonated in the air all around me, and filled me with a deep sense of order and satisfaction. It was reminiscent of large group chants I've been in that are amazingly uplifting and a comforting confirmation of the unity of mankind. Now, I hear that the incredible Sho-hondo temple has been destroyed—on purpose!

It was built to last forever and many of us donated more than we could afford toward its construction. It was supposed to usher in the new era of *kosen rufu*, world peace. Now, it's just so much rubble and dead dreams.

I think most people have heard of mantras, "Ohm" for instance. However, to get through the daily chaos in this modern fake-out world, we need something really magical!

What we need is a consciousness-changing mantra to counteract the negative influence of our demolished dreams. It needs to be something that transforms our attitude by taking our attention off the dead end of disappointment and back to the peaceful, magnificently manicured path of balance.

Luckily, my protective angels have enlightened me with a couple sacred ceremonies that do just that. So listen carefully. Imagine how you felt after one of your most serious setbacks, and then try this out. Say this mantra out loud. If you're alone, shout it—three times—each time, louder than the time before. Ready?

Here's your new, magic mantra. With reverence but energy and as much volume as possible, slowly say, "I T D O E S N 'T MATTER," or, "I T R E A L L Y D O E S N 'T M A T T E R!" Either way—It doesn't matter.

Now say it like you believe it! Now SHOUT it! You can also try, "I DON'T CARE!" You may want to improvise on this with superlatives to make it more emphatic.

Breathe deep, practice your new mantras, and know that no matter what it is, it just doesn't matter! All the fights and frustrations are just part of the game designed to provide us with challenges for our creativity and faith. We were created in the image and out of the same energy as God, the creator. The opportunity we have on Earth to draw on that unlimited creative energy for the sake of love, progress…or survival is a divine experience!

First of all, we really need to create a way out of the box of our current limitations. Almost everyone is in some sort of an uncomfortable box in one way or another, a job you don't like, no job at all, a social conflict, some sort of "bad" situation going on.

Think outside the box, and you'll be outside the box. We all have some powerful tools at our disposal that most people only casually acknowledge or don't' believe in at all. These tools start with our own desires and beliefs. That's your basic hammer. You can use it to nail a connection to your guides who are always willing to help out with any worthy cause. I asked for more business to help me make the transition between my old life and my new writing career, and the phone started ringing much more. Channeling confirmed that I was getting help from concerned souls on the other side.

You can also use the hammer of desire and belief to erect a connection to the infinite source of power, which surrounds us and everything. Thoughts are things, and your magic mantra will separate you from concern with the thoughts of others if you let it. This leaves a void that can then be filled with some powerfully constructive energy.

Your magic mantra will take the power out of life's set backs. With that "I don't care" attitude, nothing and no one can take anything from you. Maintain a good, positive intention toward your future and all who are concerned. Don't give into the darker side of emotional reactions. Remember the unified principle? Love makes all things work. Align yourself with that one power principle behind everything. Expect that things will work out for the best no matter what things look like now, and things will work out, even when we don't know how or why. In fact, I think that pretty much sums up our existence in this fake-out world.

We contemplate our good intentions and the loving universe, which can make anything possible. We take one challenge, one improvement, and one day at a time until inspiration carries us way outside the box. Of course, there's always a danger there of being perceived as maybe a little odd. That puts us in another box.

Remember your mantra: "I DON'T CARE!" With that determination, boxes always break, and we're free again.

Why should we care about the box others might see us in, or the label on the box? The box hasn't been created that can hold a soul enlightened enough to not give a second thought to what others might think.

"It just doesn't matter!" Believe it! Believe in the magic transformational power of knowing that nothing matters except our belief in our self, joy in our creations, and our sense of humor about everything else.

To New Thought and Unity
and a grateful heart

15

Thanks—The Great Purifier

…thanks is the key that opens that door to a deeper intelligence, which understands everything.

My kids argue and fight. We give each other heart attacks at work, and the world teeters on the edge of potential annihilation. Throughout it all, we grow from the laughs and hugs, and everyone eventually recovers from the trauma. It's a good trade off, and there's a lot to be grateful for! If nothing else, we can be grateful for our perspective. Since none of us are getting out of here alive with anything but our perspective, that's a blessing worth cultivating.

One of my daughters got channeled confirmation that another entity she was talking to in her head was real. Then, one day, I somehow lost about $400 out of my pocket on the way to the bank. I was up most of the night feeling stupid and worrying about the loss. I told my daughter about the problem in the morning (when I had to explain why I overslept), and at first she didn't react at all. Then she said, "It'll get better real soon." She explained that this wasn't her, but a message from her friend. She then explained where I lost it, and that a person who "looked like a bum" had found it.

I had wanted to believe that the Universe was just redistributing the wealth for purposes of which I wasn't aware, but it really helped to have this confirmed. I was grateful for a lot of things at that point. In fact, later, when I could get away and think about it all, I was inspired to tears as my thoughts spilled over to all aspects of my perceived problems and prosperity.

Generally, people do their best to do what they feel is right and necessary. We may be misled by personal concerns, faulty perceptions, fear or worry. However, we all want the same love, security, and happiness.

Seeing someone or something in the world as the enemy is a perception problem. It blinds us to the real problem and to our unlimited potential for peace and prosperity, which we would otherwise enjoy. There are an infinite number of ways to see things wrong, and basically only one way to get it right.

I was too worried about money. So it seems I needed a crash course in prosperity. Once I had crashed emotionally after the realization of losing what little I had, I was able to open up to my potential to replace that money and to the lessons of gratitude.

Fear is the enemy—"the only thing we have to fear..." as someone once said.

Or as Ralph Waldo Emerson put it, "The wise man in the storm prays to God, not for safety from danger, but from deliverance from fear. It is the storm within that endangers him, not the storm without."

As soon as trust replaces fear, we're free to create the ground under our own feet, one step at a time. It's a magical process and proof of our power over this fake-out world.

No one has the whole picture. Not knowing what someone might do, or what might happen, can cause us fear and apprehension. It might cause us to pull in and shut down. Those are all natural reactions and nothing to feel bad about. However they don't have to be the only reactions!

Natural reactions are the mechanisms the negative forces have in place to test us. Negative, mischievous entities sometimes just sit back and watch all the chaos. Don't give them the satisfaction!

The first step (which I've come back to more times than I can remember) to salvaging our lives from this vicious machine, is to choose to react out of trust and the expectation that all will be well. It's hard to trust when things seem to be going so wrong. However, when I lost that money, and for that matter, each time a marriage or career crashed or threatened to (which encompasses most of my life), the only way I could finally go on, was to trust that things could work out and try to find something for which to be grateful.

Trust makes thanks possible, and giving thanks is the great purifier! Just as fear shuts the door on understanding, **thanks is the key that opens that door to a deeper intelligence, which understands everything.** Even when we don't consciously understand, giving thanks purifies our minds and makes us feel like we understand, which is half the battle.

It also purifies our thoughts and emotions, so that the energy once used to scatter our attention and efforts can be used to create inspiration and passion for life. Thanks melts the blocks to our hearts like ice cubes in the warmth of the sun, and it lays the foundation on which to erect more tangible reasons for gratitude.

An inspired, creative life brought on by this thanks induced passion for caring and sharing fills our efforts with a self-sustaining vitality. As we work against the backdrop of darkness, our lights, charged up on creativity and passion, shine like stars in the night.

A thankful consciousness and constant good intention also makes us invulnerable to anxiety about the results of our actions. On one level, we may acknowledge pain, fear, anger etc. However, in our hearts, we're as indestructible as water flowing over and around the stones in a stream.

Kids understand their real, indestructible self so much better than adults! We can learn a lot about loyalty, devotion and faith from them. Sometimes those things seem to come as naturally to a child as breathing. Witnessing those times is like looking through a window to the kingdom of heaven. As we open that window we are blessed by the purifying fresh air of gratitude as we watch divine devotion in action.

To New Thought and Unity
and victory everyday!

16

Devotion

In the ocean of shallow emotions and self serving concerns, sometimes we're blessed by the discovery of an island of selflessness—a hero or heroin that inspires us to see a greater potential than the world usually shows us. Their devotion to something bigger than themselves exemplifies the best of this world, and inspires our hope for a better one.

A while back, I had a ram that terrorized everyone regularly. It had trapped my 12-year-old daughter in the barn, on top of some hay, for hours once before we found her. It also caused me to break my hip as I tried to avoid a run in with it on the icy ground one winter. We all learned fairly quickly to give that beast his space.

However, one day, when I was in the back yard with my two youngest daughters, the ram suddenly appeared and started moving quickly toward my three-year-old. My five-year-old looked at me, and saw I was way too far away to do anything about it. Then, this tiny little girl, with a heart much bigger than her body, charged the horned monster, waving her arms and yelling for all she was worth!

I was never so shocked and reassured by the power of love in my life! She also surprised the ram, who then took off in the opposite direction. Little Veda's instincts and follow through that day won her a gold medal in the Olympics of the heart as far as I'm concerned! She saw what had to be done and just did it! The fact that she bluffed out the beast, and came out of it unharmed, makes it an even better story.

The urge to do what's right, no matter what, is the voice of soul. How well we follow that urge in the face of danger is the test of our character. When I was in Buddhism, we had a saying that you should be willing to "follow your master into hell." Like my heroic five-year-old, all of us occasionally have to flirt with danger, or maybe even the flames of hell, as we follow the beckoning voice of soul.

Our attitude of devotion to this voice is our statement to the universe that we are not subject to the threats of this world, and our actions are proof of this triumph. Sometimes, we're rewarded with complete satisfaction by successfully accomplishing our task at hand, as Veda was with the monstrous ram. Other times just doing what's right has to be reward enough.

Either way, the mere act of listening to our heart and heeding the dictates of love and duty, stakes our claim to the higher ground. It makes us better people and the world a better place. Even when we don't win the battle at hand, each little act of courage plants a flag on another hill top. Each act of devotion to something bigger than ourselves thus helps win the war against the limitations of this world.

It's interesting that another word for devotion is worship. What we are devoted to IS what we worship. In this dualistic world, we really only have two choices. Although they manifest in many ways, one choice is faith and courage and the other is fear and discouragement. Do we commit to boundless courage, or do we give our devotion by default to the dangers of the world?

Are we going to let the horned monsters of this world claim our playground and loved ones, or are we ready to stand up against them? Courage in the face of danger may seem crazy. Still, when the day is done, "it's a craziness which comes with a calm heart and a peaceful mind," (*The Don Q Point of View* by Hunt Henion). Devotion also changes the whole moral of the story of life. Instead of just getting by, it makes each day, as long as we live, a victory!

17

Feedback

After I'd palpitated over my first few pitiful paragraphs, I paused to imagine the wondrous written work I expected to bring forth. I was basking in that glory as I showed what my creation could ultimately become to a few on the other side. They nodded in approval, to which I proudly proclaimed, "Well, I AM Hunt Henion!"

Then someone simply said, "Not always."

Like my unfinished creation, I could be something great if I could only keep myself in the right frame of mind. However, I'm not nearly always there. The gravity of this fake-out world still pulls me down.

It's amazing how much potential feedback we carry with us all the time. I occasionally run into kids who are very open about the voices they hear. My daughter has introduced me to two of her non-physical friends so far, and they've relayed some information that has proven to be amazingly accurate. A friend of this daughter also told me about her invisible friend who speaks with a Jamaican accent. Evidently, he's fun and very helpful.

However, even without spiritual guides that we consciously recognize as such, we each carry a whole array of angel emotions and demon attitudes that give us feedback. Warm feelings mean move closer. Cold ones mean move away. This internal feedback of attitudes and emotions fights constantly with each other as does our incoming feedback from the external world testing our grip on what's real.

Our minds are also set up with automatic mechanisms that act as guides in various situations. Values taught to us when we were young can act as guides, as can our knee-jerk reactions from the feedback we accumulate from the constant assault of opinions and attitudes all around us.

Making sure we actually hear these opinions correctly is another issue. Once, when we were channeling, the first thing that divine being said was, "All the things you're worrying about, you don't have to worry about any more."

So I didn't, and my business almost dwindled down to nothing! Eventually, I realized that he simply meant to not put negative emotional energy into my life. He didn't mean I didn't have anything to worry about anymore. Big difference!

Feedback can be very valuable, but sometimes so can escaping it. These are the times that reinforce the reality that each of us has a special, personal connection with our infinitely wise and powerful source. **Our own best judgment is the ultimate authority over our own lives.** That may seem a little scary, but it can also be a tremendous relief.

Feedback from fearful spots in our own minds or from meddling relatives may not be the best advice. Feedback from an angelic being who isn't blinded by physical fake-outs may be misunderstood. Sometimes we're just better off to just avoid any feedback when we can. Like everything else in this world, it's a balancing act, and harmony with the world around us hangs in the balance.

18

Harmony

Either most people are way off, or we are. That's pretty obvious! It's also pretty obvious that the earth is flat. It's all a matter of perspective.

The one standout memory from being in high school and college choir was that awesome feeling of being one with a beautiful and powerful harmony. Sometimes I tested the egotistical satisfaction of hearing my own voice over those around me. However, that was nothing compared to getting a little quieter and blending into one tone that had a resonance, which went right through me and carried me away.

It takes many voices working together to do that. No singular note, no matter how uniquely beautiful, can create harmony all by itself. Its real value is only discovered when we're able to incorporate it into a whole chord.

While on a particular spiritual path for over 20 years, I was often in a huge room, filled with hundreds of people each singing the same word, but on a different note. They often were even on a different chord. However, because the group was so big, there was still a totally amazing harmony! It all blended and was beautiful.

"In the beginning, there was the word"—one word, one name for God. All creation followed, and from where I stand, it often looks as if all hell broke loose and has been spinning out of control ever since. Still, whose job is it to control the apparent chaos, or change those who sound off key? Some people try, but because they're fighting the natural order of things, they'll never succeed.

Maybe if we could just try to blend a little, a lot of the chaos would go away all by itself. Then again, maybe the chaos we think we hear is just an illusion based on our position and perspective. It could be that if we could get far enough away from the world, it might sound even more harmonious than that room full of discordant people singing/chanting the same word on a different note.

Twelve seems to be the magic minimum number for complete harmony. In fact, harmony of all sorts always seems to break itself into twelve equal parts. There are twelve notes in an octave and twelve overtones between each note.

Having a friend or two to back us up is nice, but for serious harmony, we really need at least twelve totally different people on our side. We move through twelve signs in the zodiac to round out our perspective, and Jesus had twelve disciples. There were originally twelve tribes in Israel, and there are twelve inches in a harmonious foot.

I'm not saying an inch isn't significant on its own. However, the expression, "inching along" seems to indicate a particularly laborious slowness. No one I know wants to be laboriously slow!

Understanding and appreciating our own individualism is the first step in learning how we can best influence the unconscious clang and din of this noisy world. Fine tuning our skills and uniqueness is essential. However to really make music, we need to learn to appreciate the sounds of others no matter how difficult and unreasonable that may seem.

Once we slip into our unique, harmonious spot, so that we can no longer hear our voice above the resonating tone around us, it may feel like we've been diminished. However, that's just another fake-out of this ego-centric world. Trust the invisible conductor, and trust that when we're invisible to others, we're expressing his/her image perfectly. Besides, focusing on the harmony, which is always greater than our one lone voice, can free us from some otherwise impossible personal struggles. Something inside, perhaps an unconscious memory of home is always unsatisfied until we achieve a state of harmony with our environment.

Give in to it. All that's really lost when we blend is the chaos of disharmony. It takes discipline to see and achieve an invisible spot in a beautiful blend. It may feel like a little cage at first. Yet, it's also a profound truth that committing ourselves to the spot where we blend the best can set us free like nothing else!

19

Little Cages

When I was a little boy and first started crawling my way into mischief, my parents decided to put me in a play pen. I was supposed to play happily and stay out of trouble. That was their plan. Mine was to get continue my exploration of the world, so I broke out the first day. I'm told I actually broke one of the wooden bars.

They never tried putting me in it again, but they did get that pen out of storage when my sister came alone. They just turned the side with the hole toward the wall, and it worked fine. It worked fine for two cousins later on too. Some people are just more naturally content with their little cages than others I guess.

I've busted out of just about every cage I've ever known. Consequently, I probably now have a lot more freedom than I do anything else. Looking back at some of those "bad" situations, I can't help but wonder if I should have tried a little harder to harmonize. Maybe I could have been happy trying to play nice within the confines of the marriage or the job. Maybe I could have learned to blend back when learning something new came a lot easier.

About a year after I broke out of the pen, I stumbled into our backyard pool. I had never learned the first thing about swimming; still I bobbed to the top, and dogpaddled to the edge just like a little puppy. I've stumbled into deep water many times since then too. Sooner or later, I've always gotten my head above water. I'm not anxious to test this again, but so far I've survived, and I've learned.

> *By three methods we may learn wisdom: first, by reflection, which is noblest; second, by imitation, which is easiest; and third by experience, which is the bitterest.*
> –Confucius

I really can't think of much I've learned by imitation— the "easiest" way. Mostly, I've had to find things out for myself—the "bitterest" way possible! Taking that road tends to set us back and soften us up so that reflection comes a little easier. So I've reflected a lot! I've reflected on my responsibilities, freedom, my cages, and on my escapes. Still, "wisdom" has remained stubbornly illusive—almost as if it were also avoiding a cage.

20

Little Kids

Sometimes our light goes out but is blown into flame by another human being. Each of us owes deepest thanks to those who have rekindled this light.

–Albert Schweitzer

My light was pretty dim when I won primary custody of my little girls. The day to day handling of my business and sometimes full-time job as a substitute teacher combined with all the kid and house stuff was pretty overwhelming sometimes. Yet, the real shock and challenge came when I had time to practice that "noble" habit of reflection.

That was a light snuffer for seven years whenever I stopped to realize that I was alone with no romantic prospects in a tiny town, isolated from any possible partners and getting older every day. Yet, when I got perspective on it all, I'd realize that this little cage was probably a blessing. My daughters, who were four and five years old at the time of the divorce, and my last ex, were my anchors. They kept me from making what could have been fatal plunges. They also anchored my humility.

When the snow falls, as it does in Montana at least six months out of every year, I'd looked around at the silent, lonely, frozen world, and my heart would ache, as if bitten by the frost. I felt deserted and done-for on many such days. With the help of my little girls, I've slowly evolved out of that fake-out. Almost every day, something very innocent and special happens. They would do or say something that would make this very important parenthood time feel even more magical. They've lightened my heart and reassured me with their grins and giggles, and their growing love their whole lives.

There were days when I had to look for reasons not to check out of this world for good, and the little girls were always there to throw me a lifeline. The same thing happened in my previous marriage too. After that divorce, I got custody of my son when he was about their same age. First, he saved me, and then they renewed my rescue.

I know now that my higher self arranged to have them sent into my life after I took a detour, which voided major provisions in my life contract and extended my departure date (indefinitely) from the world. I was wandering aimlessly with the urge to leave this life at the contracted time when the kids suddenly became a bigger part of my life because of the divorce. They gave me the beginning I needed and a new purpose in this world just when it felt like I had reached my limits.

I've finally run out of little kids, but love has blossomed all around them. Their younger years taught me a lot about patience, and the years that followed built a foundation on which love has been growing ever since.

Now, life and love is sprouting, budding, and maturing all around me in a way that defies fake-outs. Love is the one thing we can count on in this world. It's our grounding and anchor to the infinite source of all blessings. It's hopeful and exciting and full of wonder and possibilities, and it brings out the little kid in all of us!

When I was actually a kid, about eleven, I started getting answers about life from a Tibetan master named Rebazar. He helped me heal from my father's death and helped me find answers to all of my questions. At one point, when I felt I had a lot of information that most didn't, I started writing down the answers. Then, when I felt the weight of ego, I threw it all away, and didn't really write again until about 40 years later. I've always wondered how things might have turned out if I handled my worries about ego some other way.

Now, my daughter is getting answers from a couple of spiritual beings whom she knows from past lives. She shares these answers with me regularly. I don't know how she'll handle this gift or what she'll have to go through because of it, but I know the little kid in me is very excited for her. She tends to ignore this resource so she can lead a more normal life, just like I did. Still, she has an open line to all the answers in the universe and her whole life ahead of her to figure out what to do with it.

Perhaps, she'll have some little kids of her own someday to blow her flicker back into a flame. I pray that they'll inspire her with new hopes and dreams and innocent happiness just as mine have for me; that they'll enlighten and humble her and that their optimism will make her less vulnerable to the heaviness of the grownup world.

Amen.

*To New Thought and Unity
— the way to true invulnerability!*

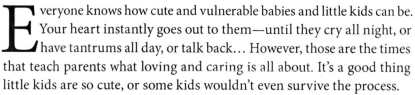

21

Vulnerability

Everyone knows how cute and vulnerable babies and little kids can be. Your heart instantly goes out to them—until they cry all night, or have tantrums all day, or talk back... However, those are the times that teach parents what loving and caring is all about. It's a good thing little kids are so cute, or some kids wouldn't even survive the process.

As we get older, some of us aren't nearly so cute anymore. Unfortunately, our vulnerabilities don't usually go away, so we have to start being pretty careful about who we rub the wrong way. One way to help keep fear about this situation at bay is to simply deny any vulnerability. That would be the ideal situation. However, as Goethe put it (in his comment about marriage), *"a confusion of the real and the ideal never goes unpunished."*

The Greek hero, Achilles, was known for being totally impervious to all onslaughts, until one day, when his vulnerability was exposed. It was such a little spot—such a small weakness that cost him his life. No wonder almost everyone today is spooked about letting their weakness show. If such a small weakness could put Achilles under, imagine what ours can do to us. Never let your vulnerabilities show! That MUST be the moral to the story!

Even to acknowledge our vulnerabilities is scary stuff. However, just like every other fear, that one is also a fake-out. It's just another smoke screen set up to hide our way home. The funny thing here is that fear about our vulnerabilities makes us even more vulnerable!

I learned that lesson repeatedly as a soldier in my past lives. However, to illustrate it best, we have to look back at the lifetime where I strayed from the light. I'm not proud of it, but as the aid to Genghis Kahn, my job was mainly to intimidate the enemy and exploit their vulnerabilities. I knew that once I could create enough fear in the enemy, our soldiers could just go cut down the opposition like so much wheat and secure the victory.

It seemed absolutely magical. I'd start with a real threat as a seed fear. Then, I'd use the tools of the trade, mostly psychological ones, to build the fear of an unbeatable monster around that seed fear. Remembering the real threat, the enemy would connect the two and get totally demoralized. They thought it was enough to go into battle and do their best with a good strategy, but it never was.

People generally just don't get it. They greatly underestimate the power of the unseen unless fear causes them to see something that just isn't there. In a world with opponents, it's essential to know what we can depend on. Weakness caused by fear of the unknown was one of the primary platforms on which we mounted our strategy.

Still, strategies and logistics are only the basics. The Kahn and I would study our vulnerabilities and reinforce them. We'd never attack, until there wasn't a single fear in the troops. We'd hide ourselves far away from danger until we were ready. Then we still wouldn't advance on any serious opponent until after I'd worked my magic on them.

Only after building up the confidence of our troupes and breaking down our opponents' with fear would we finally make our move. We were realistic and only started fights we could win, and my recollection of it is that we always won. Eventually, when Genghis had achieved enough he succumbed to a natural death. At that point, I'd had enough too, so I made a strategic retreat and I lived the rest of my days in happy anonymity in a tiny mountain community.

However, even then, I helped make the village I called home invulnerable by disposing of their enemies. People learned to steer clear of our neck of the woods. Rumor had it that our village was protected by an evil spirit. Even the villagers themselves really didn't know what was going on. Actually, it was just protected by an old but stealth warrior who knew the vulnerabilities of his friends and how to intimidate the enemy. After being in the business, working my magic for these simple people was just good recreation.

At any rate, admitting vulnerability and working with it is the first step toward any successful campaign. This may seem like a simple, pragmatic strategy, but it works on all levels. Admitting our vulnerability grounds us in what's *real* so that we don't miss any of the steps necessary to secure our *ideal*. Vulnerability is the crack in the shell around ego that allows soul to send down roots, which seek out and gather whatever our little plant needs.

Being honest about vulnerabilities opens the door and shines a light on all those dark secrets and heavy burdens we instinctively lock away. Once the door is open, the demons of fear and regret can escape. This can literally be a life saver. When we're free of the burden of fear, our load is lighter. We're more open and happy, and simply more loveable creatures—just like cute little kids again.

I used to go out on emotional limbs and worry they'd break. Often they did, and when I stopped bouncing so well, I found that being true to myself and unapologetically honest with everyone reinforces those branches. We might as well just admit our weaknesses and ignorance to ourselves and anyone else who cares before someone or some situation exposes them.

For instance, I don't know the first thing about professional sports, and I'm an idiot when it comes to mechanical things. I'm not proud of it, but I can't really hide it either. At this point, I'm probably not ever going to do anything about either of those, and I can live with that.

Not admitting weaknesses doesn't make us less vulnerable! Actually, it's the opposite. I knew a woman who often said she didn't want to go to the doctor because she was afraid of what might be found. In the meantime, she lived with worry and fear. Not smart! When the problem was finally discovered, it was worse than when she first noticed the symptoms. Today, she's no longer with us.

Guilt is another vulnerability that's not so easy to live with. People feel guilty because of their appearance, or because they don't know as much as someone else. People can feel guilty about absolutely anything, even being happy! We want to ignore our feelings of inadequacy and guilt, and hope that no one notices them. But sooner or later, they're going to be noticed, and in the meantime, we're crippled!

Guilt is the disease of a locked up mind. True, we didn't initially lock ourselves up, but we do have the key to let ourselves out. Be honest! Face your vulnerability or inadequacy. It's okay to be human!

Go ahead and open the door. Look at everything. It's never as bad as we think. It's okay to not start cleaning house right away, but there's no need to feel guilty about putting it off either. Direct that energy instead to where it will do the most good. Bask in your forgiveness of yourself for a while.

Once the attitude of honesty is put in the keyhole, talking with someone else helps. Regular meditation will also keep the light shining on all those dark corners. Notice I didn't say "occasional" meditation. Regular discipline and damage control is necessary because the doors to those dark corners of vulnerability are all on self-closing hinges. Keep an eye on them! Don't turn you back, or they'll hit you in the butt. **Never underestimate the power of the unseen.**

When we uncover our issues, fears and vulnerabilities, study them and deal with them expecting that our best will emerge from the experience, the fake-out world loses its grip on us. We take the necessary steps to shore up our important inadequacies. Then with love and acceptance of ourselves and our place in the world, we consciously commit all of our other shortcomings to the realm of things that just don't matter much anymore. This secures our link to our infinite source, voiding our vulnerability. Free of fear, we're suddenly ready live, dream and wonder...

I am the Alpha and Omega, the beginning and the end, the first and the last.

Revelations 22:13

~~~~~

A & Ω Productions

22

11:11, 13:13, & 12.21.12

Alpha is the first letter in the Greek alphabet. It's also the "probability of error" in statistics, which is a reminder that from the beginning, errors and fake-outs have been an integral part of our existence.

Omega is the last letter in the Greek alphabet. It's also used in particle physics to describe the heaviest elemental particles. Interestingly, it's also negatively charged. Of course it is! In the end of a marriage or a culture of any kind, things get really heavy and negative.

Who is it that says, "I am the Alpha and Omega?" It seems like it must be the creator of this fake-out game, who's watching it get heavier and more negative, until it finally reaches its natural conclusion. At that point, we put the pieces away, and start a new game.

I'll bet that before the creator let us loose at the beginning of this "probability of error" game, hints were scattered everywhere to help us figure things out and find our way home again; hints that are happy reminders of the divine presence, and that are actually markers of divine intervention themselves. It seems like the clocks I see lately always have triple digits on them, and I'm seeing these triple digits (4:44, 5:55 etc.) as well as 11:11, everywhere and all the time these days. How is that possible? What a good game!

Besides this highly improbable preponderance of triple digits whenever we look on clocks to remind us of how someone or something outside our system might very well have a hand in what we perceive, and perhaps even in the actual clock works of what we call life, there are also other clues to the nature of things to be found in mythology. The ancient Egyptian version of the Alpha and Omega (beginning and ending), is one being they called Atum (Ra). According to the old teachings, our goal is to become more god-like, and Atum began the becoming. His name literally means "all" and "nothing." "Beginning and ending." The philosophy of oneness of all things (and nothing) combined with a profound, simultaneous beginning and ending, in these ancient teachings, is actually pretty inescapable.

Today, we also have computers as a reminder of this oneness. One is, of course, "the beginning," but in computer talk of zeros and ones, one means "the end." 11 therefore, might mean both, the beginning and ending. 11:11 seems to reinforce that by representing the two meanings with two 11's. Also, no matter how you look at it, forward or backward, we have a simultaneous beginning and ending." Two elevens also seem to hint at a reference to our dualistic world. If we were little bits of information or code in the program of life, 11:11 might be thought of as the glitch that gives us a peak at the rest of the program.

This is all guess work, but 11:11 does seem to jump right out at you. Just like when someone calls your name, it wakes you up. And once we begin to be conscious of it, it fills us with wonder.

Are we in the eleventh hour of this 3D game? The heaviness and negativity of the world, as well as the frequency of seeing those little 11:11 wakeup calls, sure seems to hint that we are. Actually, I'd guess that we're more like in the last 11 seconds of the 11th hour.

However, what's coming isn't ever nearly as important as what is right now. For many, the future, like all unknowns, throws them into the trap of fear—the father of all fake-outs. Sometimes it's better not to prophesize, but just look at the wondrous changes in the works—in the world, and in ourselves.

Generally, people are getting more communicative and sensitive exactly the way many believe the ancient Mayans predicted. The presence of 11:11 in our consciousness seems like an element, or a least a symbol, of this new communication.

The Mayan Calendar ends on December 21, 2012 (12.21.12). In that year, the winter solstice begins at exactly 11:11 AM! I suppose it could be coincidence. But it sure feels like another of those increasingly frequent hints or reminders that we're all part of something much bigger than anything we know. Perhaps we fit into cycles we're just beginning to understand.

On the December 21, 2012, the axis of the earth will move so that it begins to point to the edge of the section of space that we've come to call Aquarius. This will be the actual beginning of The Age of Aquarius, a time of peace and enlightenment that will last for 2160 years. Then, there are five more astrological houses that also promise peace and prosperity.

It seems that as long as the earth's axis points toward the center of the galaxy, which it does for half the trip around the Procession of the Equinox (or about 13,000 years), it's like standing in the sunlight and enlightenment fills our consciousness. Then, as the earth's axis begins to point away from the center of the galaxy, mankind seems to fall asleep spiritually, and things turn more negative. At the 26,000 year mark (after one complete trip around the Procession of the Equinox), serious disruption almost always occurs. Still, that disruptive impact is just a speed-bump compared to what happens at the end of a cycle that's 1000 times larger.

Two paleontologists by the names of David Raup and John Sepkoski wrote an abstract published in 1984 by the National Academy of Sciences called, "Periodicity of Extinctions in the Geologic Past." They studied 12 extinction events. "The 12 events show a statistically significant periodicity ($P < 0.01$) with a mean interval between events of 26 million years." In other words, science is aware of 12 extinction events in our past that occur about every 26 million years. It goes on to say that only two of them were caused by meteorites, but they suspect that there are some more basic cyclical causes "related to extraterrestrial forces (solar, solar system, or galactic)."

No one knows what cyclical causes within a solar system could be indicative of further major change ahead. However, recently, science has made some very peculiar discoveries within our solar system:

The Sun has been more active since 1940 than at any time in previous 11,000–13,000 years.

Mercury has suddenly developed polar ice! How can the closest planet to the sun, which is suddenly much hotter than ever before, suddenly be freezing at the poles? It's also developing a new, much stronger, magnetic field.

Venus is suddenly 2500% brighter because of "substantive global atmospheric changes in less than 30 years."

Mars, like Earth, is experiencing "Global Warming," huge storms, and the disappearance of their polar icecaps.

Jupiter has been shown to be experiencing massive internal warming causing some to suspect it is turning into a new sun. It's also gotten over 200% brighter.

Saturn has decreased its rotational speed in the last 20 years and has been putting a huge increase in X-rays from its equator.

Uranus has had tremendous increases in brightness and global cloud activity.

Neptune has increased 40% in atmospheric brightness, and

Pluto has increased its atmospheric pressure 300%, even as Pluto continues to drift away from the Sun!

No one can adequately explain any of these changes. The most we can do is try to understand the small changes by looking at the corresponding bigger changes, and visa versa. The universal holographic implications of this connection are fascinating all by themselves!

We now know that there's an extinction/new order cycle ever 26 million years. Stepping this down a bit we find that the earth's Procession of the Equinox, which is the time it takes the earth to revolve all the way around on its tipped axis, making a complete circle in the sky, is about 26,000 years.

If we look back to when the earth was tipped in the exact direction 26,000 years ago as it is now, we see that Cro-Magnon Man roamed the earth. Stepping this cycle down further it's interesting to note that perhaps the 260 day gestation period for a human in the womb correlates to a 26,000 year gestation period of a human species.

It's also interesting that so many believe that a new sort of human is developing right now. Many have been talking about the special abilities of what they call the Indigo or Crystal children for years. The Incan elders have also recently announced the emergence of what they call "homo luminous." Some people are quick to point out the differences in the extraordinary abilities of the children they observe. However, the point here is that people are suddenly, and for the most part unexplainably, changing.

Paul Dong and Thomas E. Raffill wrote a book in 1997 entitled *China's Super Psychics*. It documents studies of children who demonstrated an ability to see flawlessly with their ears, nose, mouth, hands or feet. *Omni* magazine did their own follow-up on this. They went over there, took a page out of a book at random, crumpled it up, and put it in the armpit of one of the psychic kids, who then read ever word on that page. Their report on their study was released in their January 1985 issue.

My favorite story in the *China's Super Psychics* book is the account of an audience of several thousand who were all given a rose bud before taking their seat. A little six-year-old girl walks out on stage, waves her hand and all the rose buds open up simultaneously.

A *New York Times* article dated March 7, 2006, written by Nicholas Wade, entitled "Still Evolving, Human Genes Tell New Story," starts out: "Providing the strongest evidence yet that humans are still evolving, researchers have detected some 700 regions of the human genome where genes appear to have been reshaped..."

Western researchers have generally only been interested in the 10% of our DNA that regulates biological and emotional traits. They call the other 90%, which has recently been proven to "have been reshaped," *junk DNA*. Yet, this junk has been recently proven to respond to thought, intent and sound, which brings us back to the intelligent design theory that was thrown out shortly after Darwin made his debut.

In *The Science of Peace*, Dr. Glen Rein demonstrates how negative emotion causes DNA to contract while positive emotion causes it to expand, which enhances healing. Examples of how DNA responds to thought and words are as endless as the examples of how humans are very quickly evolving in ways that take our experience of the world to a whole new level.

Dr. Rein's research into how emotional states affect our very DNA makes me wonder about the implications of some classic psychological advice (loosely translated): *"The most important things to have are faith, hope and love; and the greatest of these is love."*

I don't think I've ever heard better guidance on how to prepare for the new, evolved world than that! It comes from I Corinthians 13:13. Hmmmm… Do you suppose that chapter and verse could be a clue to anything—an intelligent presence, a cycle, a powerful unseen causality of some sort?

11:11 stimulates our imagination and hope, just as these times test what we really choose to see and believe. 11:11, 13:13, and 12.21.12 may mean nothing to some people. To others, they may be symbols of the doorway to a greater reality. To a few of those, the faith, hope and love that those symbols inspire will be found to be reliable keys to that doorway to the infinite.

I've heard kids say, "It's "time to make a wish," when they see 11:11 or repetitive numbers on a clock. "Out of the mouths of babes…"

I don't know exactly what's going to happen at the end of the Mayan Calendar any more than I know what's going to happen at 11:11 today. Although, I'm pretty sure there are some exciting beginnings and endings just around the corner. We'll have to wait and see, but my wishes are ready!

Talking about miraculous synchronicities, when I finished this chapter, I emailed it to my wife. Later, I noticed that I just happened to send it at exactly 11:11 AM. Maybe that was just another coincidence. Or is it possible that what we think we know about probability is, in reality, just another elaborate fake-out?

23

Beginnings and Endings

ights, camera," the director points, and we have action! From the minute the lights went on in the physical universe, we've been watching and recording the action. Of course, we expect action, or we wouldn't have come to the show. We would have just stayed home enjoying eternal bliss.

Sure, we could create bliss here, and that is the stated goal. However, so far, it hasn't' been the inclination. "Been there, done that! What else is there?"

So, we are all players in a drama, tragedy, comedy or adventure. No one questions their part or the storyline until the scene is over. Then... well, you know actors—they whine, and complain about almost everything. But soon they get themselves together, ready for the next great production. All eventually agree that "The show must go on!"

Trains are wrecked. People are killed. Things explode all over the place! The audience cries, but experiences a range of emotion and examples of heroism that helps them come away with a moral and maybe some inspiration. The players improve their craft, and the critics criticize. Everyone is productively occupied, and in the end, even the players who were killed off, get up and look for their next great part—their next glorious production.

Angels stand back and watch in amazement, helping where they can when they're asked, but they generally let us play. They have a perspective we usually lose when caught up in all the drama. That perspective simply stated is, "It just ain't real!"

Sure, it feels real when we're on the stage. Good actors actually feel their part. But it's important to remember that we aren't the part we're playing. We are the actor who's had many parts, and remembering some of them might help with our current role. Its' also good to remember now and then, when people are fighting and dying, that it's just a play. It's like kids who play with toy guns running all around the yard, but then come in for lunch.

"Now kids, maybe you should find a nicer game."

"Do we have to?"

"Well, no, but…"

And so the games continue. However, more and more actors are walking off stage, and just watching. To step out of character in the wings feels like an extreme measure. However, when you want to get perspective, that's what you do. You don't withdraw from the world for the duration, but you step off stage now and then.

If we simply smile, for instance (and repeat our magic mantra in our minds), when something bad happens, it may feel really strange. React happily in upsetting situations long enough and you'll question your own sanity. You'll want to come back to center. However, that middle path isn't what it used to be. When there's no reasonable, moderate part to play, not playing at all is the only answer. So we sit, smiling in the wings, waiting for the show to change, or as Jessie put it, waiting "for the Earth to split," so those who are attached to all the drama can continue those plays, while others of us move on.

Jessie told me once when I was enmeshed in a custody battle to "Bless all the players." If we really do believe that we're all One, and it's all good, then this is the only reasonable attitude. Reasonable or not for now, it sure does feel good, and with all the magic in the air these days, I am inclined to believe that it's reasonable.

A new script is written. Plenty of players are ready. When the set finally is broken down and cleared off, there'll be no turning back. We'll all really begin to feel our parts and inspire others to do the same. Those pretenders controlling center stage will just have to take their act elsewhere.

First, the curtain will come down on the economy, then the political and social structure. Neighbors will finally get to know each other. The old stars will try to protect themselves at our expense, but earth changes will put a quick end of their selfish plans (and backup plans). When the dust clears, people will take inventory and pick one of two paths. One path leads to a reestablishment of the old systems but in a more enlightened way. The other leads to more magic than most ever dreamed possible. Lights will suddenly illumine the stage of a whole new world entirely beyond the illusion of limits.

To New Thought and Unity
The new show must go on!

24

View from the Wings

The bright lights on stage blind almost everyone to everything except the play at hand. Fortunately, I was blessed with having my main character killed off early on in the current show. When my contract was up, I just took walk-on parts, which weren't much to get excited about. However, what is worth getting excited about is the view from the wings.

People here aren't caught up in all the illusion. They speak honestly without any expectations of applause. Everything an actor on stage says is from his/her limited perspective of the scene. Those in the wings, who aren't burdened with a part to play most of the time, can see things as they really are.

From the wings, we can see characters rise from the dead. We see them reunited with their families. We can see when sets get scrapped, and know that it was still a good show.

From the wings, we can see the big story behind all the plots, and clues to all the pain and conflict. We see actors, who, in one way or another, play a part we've played at one time or another.

There was the vulnerable little girl who wanted to never be vulnerable again. There was the battle-weary warrior who let down the intensity of his guard just enough to end his life of killing. There was the Japanese lord who had nothing better to do than write poetry all day, and a Greek who wrote tragedies (stories told in *The Don Q Point of View* by yours truly).

There was the murderer and the murdered, and each step out of one conflict was a step into another. Each major set change left the key players with a new wound and a new fear: A fear of being taken advantage of or a fear of taking advantage; a fear of letting down his guard, a fear of failure, and a fear of success.

The wheel goes around and the plays go on. Successes lead to failures, and failures lead to grounding. That's when we're free again to look up to the big blue sky and hear the singing birds, and appreciate beauty by contrast. Seeing the beauty once again inspires us to feel the love that runs the show behind the scenes. This triggers the instinct to get involved again, a little wiser, and feeling EVERYTHING a little deeper.

Each time I take on a new role, I go deeper into the vat of earthly experiences that color me like a rag being dyed first blue then red, happy, then mad; then every other color with increasing passion, and then back again! The point of this whole rainbow world can only be seen from the wings. Sometimes, I swear I can see myself coming when I'm going. At those times, I remind myself that the fears aren't necessary, and anguish is definitely not necessary.

After marriage number three, I asked my guides to never let me make another mistake like that again. I had some amazing near misses since then, but the guardian of bad marriages always made sure I had a terrible experience just in the nick of time to avoid a terrible mistake. I've come to think of this guardian, who brings these bad experiences, as a very good friend.

I don't expect obviously good things to always happen, but when we can see bad experiences as a matter of choice and a way of avoiding much worse experiences, fear eases and wounds heal some. Sometimes we choose to join the oneness by giving up an advantage. Other times we get to give up a disadvantage.

From the wings, both of those turning points look the same. They're simply steps taken from a desire to bring love, compassion and a sense of unity to ourselves and/or others.

Choosing the lesser of two evils in the pursuit of the ultimate good is often what life in this fake-out world is all about. We could be sitting in the audience with the heavenly hosts, out of harms way, but where's the fun in that? Where's the love in that?

Whether the boy gets the girl or however the drama and plots resolve, it really doesn't matter much. From the wings we can see that the most important thing isn't any of the action, but what it all means to the actor, because that's what will determine what will happen next.

Back stage is the whole truth of what's actually behind all the motion and commotion in the limelight. Things are much calmer there. Everyone should get a look back stage now and then just to put the action on stage in perspective.

There are a couple people cueing the actors. There's someone controlling the curtain, and there are tech types running around doing who knows what. I think the most interesting thing though is watching the actors prepare for their next scene or production.

Of course, the next production isn't real until it's on stage, but there are quite a few of us who are excited about it. We sit back here drinking tea and having our snacks in a little bubble of bliss, totally removed from the action on stage. Compared to those who are all caught up in the performance, we must seem like we're really out of it.

Actors feel SO important, and everyone else is nobody to them. What we talk about is unimportant since it doesn't involve their play. They think we're delusional. Yet, our visions drive the creative process that's developing the next great production. Everyone has their own ideas and we compare notes by the water cooler or off in the corners.

All the actors see are a few nobodies sitting in dark corners offstage. However, for many of us nobodies, the action on stage is pretty insignificant compared to our plan for the next production. It'll be a play to end all plays.

We're going to get rid of all the petty conflicts. In fact, we're going to write antagonists out of the plot all together. Our production will be all about creative construction, instead of the endless battle for it!

The BIG Fake-Out

As soon as the current play's over, we need to strike the old set. Personally, I'd like to burn it, but I'm sure others will want it again. So we'll just move on and leave them to their old props and plots.

Interested in auditioning for the new production? Think you might like to hit the road with the crew from the wings? Just look backstage for the person holding the bubble of bliss open for you.

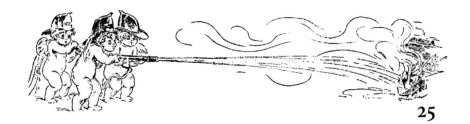

25

Endings and Beginnings

The fire is now out on the disappointment of my life, but I can still smell the smoldering of my hopes that went up in smoke. I came into this world contracted to a romantic relationship that was literally made in heaven. I met and recognized her after taking another fork in the road, which led me into unchartered territory and almost off the edge of the Earth. I wandered lost and lonely for about two decades, trying to believe that the sun still shined somewhere above all the smoke, before I made a new beginning. I really didn't think I was going to ever find a fresh start that would make sense out of it all. Yet, one day it was just there.

Knowing that there are blue skies up there somewhere is small consolation to those who've lost their jobs, homes, businesses, loved ones or health to the ways of the world, one way or another. We can't always watch from the wings. Living life is, after all, why we are here!

Also, to say it isn't real when it feels so real, will often just engender more anger than it does a peaceful perspective. Even those who haven't personally lost much to the unwinding of our economic and social systems must be looking around and wondering why in God's name, those in power are polluting our air, water, food and our lives in every way imaginable. Why are they poisoning the world we all live in with harmful chemicals, radioactivity and endless lies?

Natural climate changes and manipulation of the weather, disease, politics, and the growing arrogance of those in power.... There are probably a dozen different developing scenarios that could very likely bring about the end of the world as we know it. Why have things gotten so out of control?

In the words of Lao-tzu, the father of Taoism, *To be worn out is to be renewed.*

In the words of Hunt Henion, the self-proclaimed father of fake-out survival, *Things are being pushed to the edge of destruction because a miraculous recovery, or maybe even a resurrection from the dead, will be such an amazing experience and such a great story to tell later!*

When this current socioeconomic world finally goes through the purification process many of us have been going through, many old, respected institutions will die. New ones will then be reborn from the ashes. The systems we've come to rely on will wear out entirely. Then, as Lao-tzu put it, *be renewed.*

Lao-tzu is also the one who said, *A journey of a thousand miles begins with a single step.* However, what steps are even worth taking at this point? When we plant seeds, the gardeners in charge poison them. To give up is apathetic, but to keep trying against impossible odds seems pretty dumb too.

When I start to question the value of all my worthless actions and merit-less hopes, I remember the story of a monk who came to a beach where starfish had washed up out of reach of the normal tides. You've probably heard this old story, but I love it so here it goes:

The starfish were all over the place, and he couldn't possible save them all, but still he was calmly going about rescuing the ones he could. His disciple asked him, *Master, in the grand scheme of things, what difference does it make that you rescue a few starfish?*

The monk replied, *It may not matter in the grand scheme of things, but it matters to the starfish I save.*

So what are we supposed to do to help? The beauty of the answer to that question is that it can't even be put in terms of current conventional wisdom. I don't think there are any possible plans that couldn't be shot down by someone. Still, helping the few starfish we can, does feed our soul. The more it's fed, the more it can sink roots into the earth wherever soul finds us. Then, as we nurture the needs of the soul seed, it grows, reproduces, and multiplies, empowering a whole new way of life.

Even now, under the canopy of old growth, little sprouts of new life are growing unnoticed. As the old giants die of decay or disease, this new life is quietly preparing to flourish. This "tragic" ending is actually a fresh beginning for all us little sprouts.

You know it. The decaying old trees know it! And if you listen carefully, through the cheers of the angels, you can hear the deep baritone chuckles of old Alpha Omega himself.

*To New Thought and Unity
for a better view of Heaven!*

26

The Thinning Veil

You will hear of wars and rumors of wars, but see to it that you are not alarmed. Such things must happen...
                                          –Matthew 24:6

Why must such things happen?

Because it is written in the script of the Fake-Out-Land! It's necessary to maintain the balance and to draw the line between those who are quick to fight and those who will do anything to avoid it. Even as the shift hits the fan and all Hell breaks loose, so does all of Heaven. It's all setting the stage for a really flashy finish!

As catastrophes increase, so does the knowledge of the divine spark in each of us, which responds to those in trouble. Heartfelt prayers connect all like-minded souls. Angels respond by bringing even more love and hope down into the clouds of confusion.

Still, fake-outs are everywhere. On one side we have those who are consumed with fear and worry. This corrosive energy rusts the buckets of blessings so that they empty through the leaks as fast as we can fill them.

On the other side, we have those who, for one reason or another, live with an aloof sense of superiority. These people tend to force feed their insights to anyone who'll stand still for it. Whether they pop illusions with pointed truths, suffocate people under a blanket of enlightenment, or simply define the parameters of their air tight illusion, the result is still the same. The angels of love and hope retreat as these do-gooders attack, trying to bully their vision of the new world into the mind of one ignorant soul at a time.

The wisdom behind not trying to save the world is illusive until you pretend you're from somewhere else. Actually, that's not too far of a stretch for a lot of us. Remember the *Star Trek* "prime directive" of non-interference? The reason to not interfere isn't exactly just because people will eventually discover what they need all by themselves and be fine without your help. It's also not because they'll feel so much better about themselves after they learn and accomplish what they need to on their own. That eventual "feel good" factor probably isn't really worth all the suffering in the meantime.

One main idea behind non-interference is that a path of self determination is sustainable, whereas just giving someone some technology or truth that they aren't close to discovering on their own breaks their forward progress. It also spoils them into wanting to wait for their next easy fix. Still, I'm sure you'll all recognize that principle from your basic study of "Inter-species Relations 101."

However, one reason for non-interference, which most people don't realize, has to do with the fact that we all contracted to live within a certain envelope of ignorance before being born into the human race. In other words, **fake-outs are an important and sacred part of the human condition. In fact, they are the framework behind the structure we all have come to know and love as "life!"**

There'd be no wonder if there was no ignorance. So, to power up our souls with wonder, the physical realm, along with its closely guarded borders of ignorance, was created. This system of ignorance, which defines the structure on which all human life is based IS THE *BIG Fake-out.*

The system is in place for the individual's best interest, but it also plays an important part in maintaining the natural balance of this world. Simple people who react in all the normal ways, just taking one day at a time, trying to do the best they can in the world they know, are the salt of the earth. Some will find themselves on the egotistical side of the line and others find themselves on the worrying side. Still, taken together, they provide balance. They are the mountains and trees that hold the earth together, and they are as beautiful as sunset over a fire zone.

Besides the fact that giving respect is generally wiser than interfering with the individual, it's also wiser for the world right now. While the universe raises the vibration of the earth and her people, and tinkers with the physics of the physical realm, these *salt-of-the-earth people* are an established, constant parameter. You don't want to mess with the constant parameters while underlying forces are being tweaked.

Another way to look at it is, while Mother Earth paces and crouches, cramps and dilates, preparing to give birth; these simple people give her peace and help prevent a premature birth. At times, we can see the beautiful face of the baby through the veil of its *bag of waters.* It's developing and growing in those holy waters, and it won't be long now until that veil breaks. As anxious as we all are for enlightenment to spill out all over the place, the timing has to be just right, and we need to be patient with the process.

In the meantime, as the veil between this world and the next one thins, we enjoy quicker healings of body, mind and soul. Channeling and telepathy are much more common. Synchronicity, like 11:11, (today's date, incidentally) is becoming an almost constant reassurance, especially appreciated now that most of our comfortable fake-outs, such as material security are vanishing.

The Earth is proving to not be nearly as rock-hard and the firmament not nearly as firm as we once thought. The Earth shakes, traditions and beliefs die, and conventional wisdom gives way to new insights and new illusions. Illusions quickly turn to disillusionment, leading to one realization: If nothing else is real, at least I AM. I KNOW I AM!

No matter how many times the rug is pulled out from under us, the one thing that is left, although bruised and battered, disillusioned and/or enlightened, is us—human souls in the bloodstream of something bigger than we can possibly imagine. We can't fight the flow, and when the veil finally breaks, who knows, all of Heaven and Earth may just fall away! Still, we'll be here somewhere, and you'll find me canoeing for all I'm worth to the heart of things.

27

The Heart of Things

There's a special place in the human heart that connects us in a very personal way to the universal heart. It's such a private place that when it's even touched during surgery, the patient instantly dies. No outsider belongs there, but to the individual, it's the most special place in the world. It's the place where we know all we need to know, and satisfaction is complete. Angels and all peaceful souls call it home, and it's the source of all miracles.

The Hebrew tradition calls this sacred place the *secret chamber of the heart*. The Upanishads, the Hindu holy writings, call it the *tiny place within the heart*. From this spot, we don't see anything or anyone as separate from ourselves. So, of course, we wouldn't hurt anyone on purpose any more than we'd intentionally harm ourselves.

When people believe they need to fight and kill for the things of the heart, they are simply mucked down in a mental puddle of illusion. Harming another to bring about a good result is never the conclusion of the heart. Yet the world has been submerged for eons in these muddy, mental, puddles.

When you pick up a hose that has been buried for years in mud and turn on the water, mud is going to come out. Mud went in, so mud will have to come out. But take heart. The clear water is coming!

In the meantime, the mud is good for the garden too. It's from the earth, just like the water. There's nutrition in that mud, and lessons to be learned in tolerating it. In the heart of things, all people and things are tolerated and accepted with equal value. There are no enemies, no conflict, and no battle.

Luckily, those who have an affinity for those things can't get across the border to the refined worlds, to do there what they've done here. To get to the pure heart of things, you have to change planes so many times that you eventually lose your luggage.

Personally, I think I'd rather go in a canoe than on a plane. Still anger, greed, lust, vanity and attachment are all going to get either washed overboard or lost in transit. When we finally step through the door to the heart of our heart, we do so empty handed, with nothing but peace, our God-given creativity and free choice, which are the seeds for our next great adventure!

Even now, the things that used to be rock solid such as work and family, economic and social order, are all swirling in the wind around us. Many still assume that they're solid, but they just haven't looked closely lately. Some little kids are solid, but other than that, the only things that'll be left when the swirling stops are the things of the heart.

Many people aren't so anxious to lose all they've worked so hard for. That's not a problem. Going to the peaceful heart of things is just one option. There are always plenty of battles to be fought elsewhere in the body of God—glorious battles, for which the supply of enemies is as infinite as the number of fake-outs in the physical world.

28

The Final Battle

*"When the final battle comes, it won't be with any evil force
we've come to hate, but with our belief in one."*

Someone had blundered:
Theirs not to make reply,
Theirs but to do & die…

Storm'd at with shot & shell,
Boldly they rode & well,
Into the jaws of Death,
Into the mouth of Hell…

Cannon to right of them,
Cannon to left of them,
Cannon behind them
Volley'd & thunder'd;
Storm'd at with shot & shell,
While horse & hero fell,
They that had fought so well
Came thro' the jaws of Death
Back from the mouth of Hell…

When can their glory fade?
O the wild charge they made!

From "Charge of the Light Brigade," written by Alfred, Lord Tennyson while he was a Poet Laureate. His expressed task was to manipulate public opinion to glorify the lives of the men in the Light Brigade after they were led in the wrong direction during a military blunder.

When I discover occasions like this of leaders directing people in the wrong direction, it hits all my hot buttons. One day, I asked my guides why. Suddenly, I saw myself on the steps of a pyramid talking to a crowd. That didn't explain a lot to me, but my first question for which I wanted a direct answer in channeling did. I asked if this really happened and if so, if it was back in ancient Egypt. By confirming that is was a true vision, he evidently gave my suppressed memories permission to come out. Then, when he said that it occurred in the Ohio Valley of North America about 50,000 years ago, that really primed my memory pump.

As I focused on this, I saw myself talking about the unity of all people with each other, nature, and our source. I saw myself leading private discussions on how to cooperate with this mystic unity in ways that result in magical transformations. However, over time, I lost my crowd. People were becoming less interested in how they fit in into the grand unity of all things, and more interested in discovering what was theirs alone.

Once that started, everyone began wanting flashy personal success, and they grew more willing to do anything for it. I came down from the pyramid and walked among the people until I got caught up in personal pursuits too. My seed karma was trying to turn the tide on this growing movement away from unity and harmony. That led to defeat and delusion, and what I know today as my biggest pet peeve.

Serving your own ego is one thing, but fooling others in ways which diminish them and feed the controlling egos, still just makes me furious. I'm learning to get a grip. That's the spiritual way. However, I'm pretty sensitive to the big egos taking over at the expense of everyone else.

The "Charge of the Light Brigade" is just one example from history of rulers pushing all they can in the wrong direction. They sent their soldiers in the wrong direction, and then they sent every one else's perception of that event in the wrong direction with PR and rhetoric.

Even successful conquests always destroy peace for the sake of an empire, which eventually crumbles and throws its citizens back into chaos. This cycle of chaos and conquest has led to some creative explanations to appease and control the people—all of which always directs everyone away from their personal relationship with the limitless nature of life.

My favorite example of this conquest of land and mind goes back to the Roman Empire and the beginnings of the Catholic Church. Less than 400 years after Rome crucified Jesus, those who claimed allegiances to him were in power and the old Roman Empire was crumbling. Could that be proof that God was on their side? Unfortunately, history indicates that it was more a matter of human "sleight of hand," than it was the hand of God.

The story of the Catholic Church begins with an account of the conversion of Emperor Constantine. His mother, Helen was a Christian most of his life. Still Constantine never converted until he was 40 years old. We also know that he still kept the sun god, *Sol Invictus,* on his coins until 321, which is 19 years after he supposedly converted to Christianity. Still, it's possible that he was a sincere convert.

However, as Peter Brown, one of the most reliable ancient historians points out:

> The conversion of a Roman emperor to Christianity, of Constantine in 312, might not have happened—or, if it had, it would have taken on a totally different meaning—if it had not been preceded, for two generations, by the conversion of Christianity to the culture and ideals of the Roman world.
> –Peter Brown, *The World of Late Antiquity, AD 150–750*, London and New York, 1971, p. 82

The message of love and forgiveness of the early Christians was pretty much lost in the perception of an angry god after Paul began his preaching of apocalyptic expectations about 50 AD. Over the next couple hundred years, that message grew into a monster. By the time Constantine came into power, Christianity was fairly compatible with the fear tactics and brutality of the Roman Empire.

Constantine's alliance with the Catholic Church was really the formation of a new governing class. The bishops of Italy became the heirs of the Roman Senate, and the bishop of Rome was suddenly the Emperor's successor. In return, the bishops used their monks as thugs to ransack houses, destroy idols and create fear, making the people easier to control.

Making the Catholic Church the only lawful religion (a law punishable by death) fit nicely into the Roman time-honored tradition of terrorizing inferiors by their superiors. The conqueror Constantine set himself up as the head of the Catholic Church in 324, securing complete control of his new power structure. Still, that absolute physical control wasn't enough. The mission of the new administration was to convince their subjects that theirs was a holy war.

Shortly after Constantine got this ball rolling, Augustine ran with it. He created to doctrine of *Cognite intrare*, or "compel them to enter." This is justified by Luke 14:23: *Compel people to come in! By threats of the wrath of God, the Father draws souls to the Son.*

Augustine was sainted for all the PR work he did promoting Constantine's vision of a world-wide power structure. From where he sat as the bishop of Hippo, in Algeria, Augustine became famous for coining convenient concepts. For instance, he was the first to discuss the concept of *original sin*. Constantine never thought of it when he was putting together his Bible, and to this day those words are nowhere to be found in either the Old or New Testaments. Nor are the words *ancestral sin*, which is the Eastern Orthodox wording for the same concept.

Augustine just figured it all out himself. I suppose God could have given the saint a P.S. to the holy book he entrusted Constantine to compile for him. Still, however that revelation occurred, it worked like a charm for Constantine's priests.

The introduction of original sin into their religious formula was key in not only explaining why the people suffered (after being conquered continuously throughout all of recorded history), but it also created the need for a paid priest craft to help people deal with this mysterious, newly discovered, burden. By shifting the blame for hardships from their conquerors to the people's own innate inadequacy, Augustine removed animosity and a lot of the opposition while at the same time cementing in the subservient role of the masses to their new (supposedly holy), elite. Brilliant!

Augustine is also the one who coined the concept of a *"just war,"* so any remaining opposition could be dealt with expediently without harming the ruler's image. Then, in his biggest stroke of genius, as Rome fell, he counseled his following about "The Spiritual City of God," which would never fall. This subliminally usurped the power from the crumbling Roman Empire, transferring it to the Roman Catholic Church, which defined itself as a free agent, obligated to no one but a God, who conveniently only spoke to them.

Walled, mountain top kingdoms may fall, but building an empire in the minds of men took the age-old practice of conquering to a whole new level. From this impenetrable fortress, the monster of the Catholic Empire sent out tentacles in all directions. They formed strategic alliances with every political power of the day.

Letting theses various political structures do their dirty work, the Church cleaned up its image a bit so that the extent of their power was undetected by many. Their program of mind manipulation and collusion with merciless rulers was an extremely successful strategy. After about 1500 years of overt and covert operations eliminating anyone who didn't whole-heartedly accept their teachings, their "holy" image grew fairly secure.

They seized control when they could and maneuvered the rest of the time stealthy behind the scenes (just like Genghis Kahn's aid did) in order to intimidate and control their population targets. In both cases, opponents were thrown off balance and conquered before they even knew what they were up against.

Augustine was a good man, but he saw the people's vulnerability and just couldn't help exploiting it. Guilt was the crack in the collective consciousness that he discovered, widened, and used to his advantage. The intimidation that he set in motion set the stage for the growth of the most powerful empire and one of the biggest fake-outs this world has ever known.

This all just goes to show that spin doctoring by rulers was by no means a new art when Tennyson wrote his famous poem. It also stands to reason that the enemies and evil forces that we've been indoctrinated by the powers that be for hundreds of generations to hate may not actually be our ultimate enemy. We've been pretty gullible so far, but at some point, mankind is going to wake up and realize that the source of our conflict isn't because of some distant enemy or ancient ancestor.

Ours is not to *"question why."* We're supposed to just *"do and die."* You've got to admire that spirit and bravery, that total devotion to the game!

However, charging into the *"jaws of death"* to take on the enemy seems somewhat less glorious when you stop to remember that everyone in the one body of God is really on the same side, at least until we're fooled into thinking that we aren't. Also, when you remember that soul is indestructible, death becomes a more of an inconvenience than a tragedy. A needless death is still more stupid than it is heroic. Yet it's interesting how both Church and State have endeavored spin their selfish claim on human life into an honorable tradition.

It's anti-climatic and un-patriotic to pop the bubble of glory (releasing nothing but hot air) around our *just wars*. After hearing Tennyson's inspiring poem, who wouldn't want to charge wildly into war for the glorious motives we want so much to accept? It's exciting, empowering, and it's in stark contrast to the state of peaceful cooperation from which we all originally came.

That's why the games began and why they continue so fiercely today. Our fearless leaders desperately do all they can to keep our attention from drifting to our similarities with the enemy. "Sympathy with the enemy" has been built up to be treason against the country and sacrilege against

God's chosen people because the PTB's (powers that be) have to keep the spotlight on the play they're directing.

From the wings though, I can't help wondering if maybe instead of leaving our bodies on the battle field, if it might not be better to simply go home, so our kids don't have to try to make it through this glorious world without us! Vicious battles are continuously waged on every front, and still new enemies keep appearing like ducks in a shooting gallery. As soon as you hit one, another one pops up. They tell us, for the sake of your country and the world, line up to do your duty and shoot those damn ducks!

Well, that game is getting a little old. **When the final battle comes, it won't be with any evil force we've come to hate, but with our belief in one.**

On that quiet morning after…, when the entire circle of ducks goes unmolested, the shooting gallery will close, and the lights will shine on a new attraction. Solders will lay down their guns, and commanders will throw up their hands. They'll warn and worry everyone they can; then they'll curse their troops.

Still…

> Glory will not fade from our illustrious Light Brigade,
> Who've just returned "from the mouth of Hell."
>
> They'll ride in peace on a mission well paid,
> AWAY from those who "blundered" so well!

To New Thought and Unity
for a better perspective

29

Flowers from the Ashes

We can pave over nature, still dandelions will emerge from the cracks. Our best creations may burn to the ground. Still, new life, bright and green, sprouts quickly from under the rubble. Life courses continuously through the earth and through our own limitless nature proving over and over that destruction is simply a passing illusion.

Sometimes nature, in its enthusiasm to express itself actually helps with the destruction, as in the case of plants growing up through the concrete. There are several old, dead stumps on our property that have tiny, little trees growing out of them. I watch these little trees everyday, just waiting for the moment they become strong enough to break down what's left of the old tree, and stand forth in their own right. Growth is slow, but life is persistent!

> *What matters death? For each time a knight falls, he shall*
> *rise again and woe to the wicked!*
> –Don Quixote in *Man of La Mancha* by Dale Wasserman

Whether that knight actually gets up to fight "the unbeatable foe" again himself, or if his spirit is renewed in another, the lesson of life flowing constantly from the infinite source is the same. As we reach for the "unreachable star," it supports us. As we fight our losing battles, it comforts us. Then, as we finally look into the face of our enemy and see the indestructible nature of life expressing itself even there, this awareness of our one life blesses uswith a victory, snatched right from the jaws of our defeat!

I love stories about renewal or resurrection. Everyone's familiar with the story of the resurrection of Jesus. However, there are quite a few more. In Greek mythology, Adonis was said to have been gored to death by a boar. Then he resurrected. Osiris, according to legend, was an immortal who lived and ruled in predynastic Egypt. He was slain by his brother, Set, who knew he couldn't actually kill him since he was immortal. So, so after he murdered him, he cut his body up into 14 pieces and scattered them all over Egypt. His wife, Isis, found all the pieces, and after putting them back together, he came back to life—as the story goes. Then there's Attis, whose birth was caused by eating fruit. (Hmmm... You think maybe his parents were Adam and Eve?) When he died he came back as a pine tree! Then there's Krishna, who supposedly didn't even die before he ascended!

There's also the biblical story about what happens to all people at the end of time. If at some point, everyone who has ever lived in this world suddenly rises from their graves, doesn't that make an interesting point about how connected and interdependent we are as a people? It also hints at the nature of time and the possibility of it ending as we know it.

However, usually those aren't the points of the story. Fear of judgment and everlasting damnation kind of shuts off all the rest of the questioning. Personally, I can hardly wait until the ending times when people wake up from their anger and fear induced stupors, arise from their walking death, and face what they've created.

I'll bet there are special plans already set up for those who instigate and profit from fear. Maybe they'll come to personally know fear. Maybe failure will help them learn something about their connection to the rest of life. I expect if a universal "judgment day" came, it would work the same way as any other end of life experience. The notions that we can cheat others or the rules of life would be exposed for the illusions that they are.

Facing our mistakes is sort of the point to life. Being afraid of dealing with the mess we've created, or trying to scheme our way out of it doesn't work in the long run. The desire to find an angle to exempt ourselves from the basic plan of life, e.g., to "get rich quick," or get to Heaven quick and easy, reveals vulnerabilities that con artists use against us whenever possible.

Like everyone else, I rise from a blissful death every morning and face the messes and successes I created the previous day. It's nothing to dread or fear. It's not like we're going to burn in hell FOREVER! A quick singe now and then is usually enough for most of us. It wakes us up, and motivates us to take care of things, so we can enjoy the new day!

I know from plenty of first hand experience how demoralizing it is when our best dreams go up in smoke leaving nothing but dangerous rubble to clean up. However, what got incinerated was just a dream. Time after time we get up, brush ourselves off, clean up the mess, and resurrect a little hope along with a new, better perspective. **Since our whole mission in the fake-out world is to gain that perspective, we're actually much more successful than most ever imagine.**

Reality is what flowers in the ashes—kids from a ruined marriage, for instance. Illusion is what might have been, and burns up all around us as we play with fire.

As we ascend from the ashy pits, resurrecting like the Phoenix from one death after another, one point becomes unmistakably clear. Life goes on and on, in darkness and in light, constantly balancing our goals and fine tuning our outlook.

To New Thought and Unity
for a better perspective

30

Outlook

Despite the popular propaganda to the contrary, Hell doesn't last forever. It gets our attention, and after a little attitude adjustment, we're back in the game. We want to stay out of trouble, but don't want to miss any good opportunities either. So, we look out—for danger, for opportunities, and for just about everything we can that's really important!

This is another case where simple folk have it hands down over those of us who tend to think too much. Because, even when we're looking in with imagination and hope, we're still looking inward, and we just aren't looking out!

Clunk! Another hit to the head, and I'm back on my butt wondering why a good thoughtful person like me keeps getting knocked down by life. Could it maybe be that my attention isn't always where it should be? Could it be that maybe I should just watch where I'm going better?

A tiny little home on stilts stands on top of the highest hill in the center of our little rural county. You can see for many miles in every direction from the windows of that little house. The woman who lives there watches out for fires. However, when I was there, I was more interested in her little home than her job. I looked around wondering about the daily routines and lack of conveniences. It was easy to get carried away with wondering about all sorts of things, but when I realized I was missing something, I looked up.

The views were magnificent! From the balcony, you can feel the wind on your face, and smell the pine trees, hear the birds sing, and watch the eagles soar. The forest has stories! Huge trees split by lightening, streams cutting new paths, squirrels scurrying busily and playfully… So much has happened and is happening, and I would have missed it all if I hadn't looked up and out!

As I stood still breathing the pine scented air, and looking at the trees and sky, I knew that I was part of it. Suddenly, I wasn't looking out from my little isolated body, but was a part of the infinitely bigger body all around me. With this outlook, which isn't so much looking out as it is being out, everything makes sense. Everything is beautiful, and all of life's little fake-outs can't touch us.

At one of his seminars, Drunvalo Melchizedek said something like; "the biggest fake-out (maybe that wasn't his exact word), the granddaddy of them all, is that we are trapped behind a pair of eyes looking out into the world that appears to be totally separate from ourselves."

This IS the perspective we learn in the physical world. Yet when we climb to the lookout tower, and spend a little time just taking in the scenery, we expand all our personal barriers, and that granddaddy of all fake-outs loses its grip on us.

We don't actually lose ourselves as one misconception of Nirvana teaches. We'll always have our own perspective! However, when we put our personal perspective in the perspective of what we're all part of, and not just looking at, smiles are suddenly deeper. They reach every cell of our body with the sense of completion and joy. Suddenly outlook isn't an issue at all. There ARE NO issues, no problems, and soul is finally free to soar.

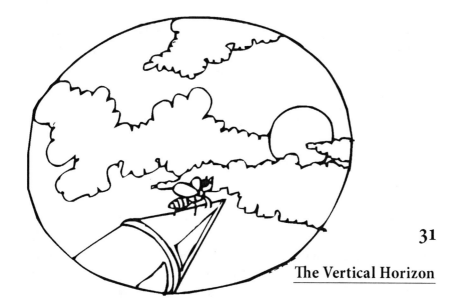

31

The Vertical Horizon

As I sit pondering my past and future, like a bug on a rocket, engines vibrating under me, all my old questions float across my mind: "How crazy are you!?" "What are you doing here?" "Are you sure?"

Still, the countdown to blastoff continues:

Five. Out of my latest mess and into the cockpit, not sure where I'm going, and a little leery of the bomb about to go off under my butt.

We've dined on the "knowledge of good and evil" like flies on manure since the dawn of time! It's caused nausea in those we call criminals, and it's been regurgitated by authorities of all kinds.

Good and bad is a profoundly simple concept, but we've complicated it with what's seemed like endless games. For many millennia, we ate our fill and played our games. We learned some lessons through success, but more through the pain of fake-outs. We let the universe work its worst on purpose so the lesson would take. Then we went along with things because we forgot we had a choice.

Four. One last check to make sure that we're clear of all those non-love-based ties.

Somehow we survived all the chaos. We should have that concept of "good and bad" down by now. We should also begin to remember soon that we have a choice to leave it all behind!

Three. Release of personal prejudices and give amnesty to all enemies.

I desperately and adamantly surrender to the Universe! I acknowledge my oneness even with those who work at cross purposes to me. I also know that's a biggie, so I'm buckling up now.

Two. Release attachment to all preferences.

I'm okay leaving my plans behind for the sake of getting to a better place. This isn't just another phase where we mellow for a while, tending our wounds; then when we can, run right back into the game. It's time to say goodbye forever to our old friends: anger, greed, lust, vanity, and the stickiest one of all, attachment. With those bindings unclamped, we've got the green light!

One. When the countdown is complete, that dead weight will be dumped!

Some people will float away like balloons without ballast. Others will absolutely blast out of the realm of power and persuasion, following their star charts to the home of heartfelt creation and cooperation. Some will never be subject to the gravity of the old situations again. That is the goal. So program that trajectory with hope and a prayer.

Check those ties one last time. There's a fond nostalgia for those familiar, old ways. Fighting can feel good sometimes. It can make you feel alive, but it can also do a lot of damage. Remember all the children who didn't really have a chance in this world, and who gave their lives to build our hearts to the point where we can sit here today. For their sake, let the countdown proceed!

Zero! Relax and resolve to let the blessing of peace blast us away from the illusion of limits once and for all. Take a deep breath, and have a good trip!

32

Happy Endings

When I was about 12 years old, I suddenly realized that my image of a preacher had changed and that I could no longer see myself doing that job. Suddenly, I was confused about how I fit into the world again and worried about what was going to happen to me. My inner guide told me simply, *"Everyone ends up where they belong."*

That was comforting even though I didn't know how long it would take, or where I belonged. Since then, I've had many hopes, and have had many hopes dashed. I don't know how far I am from the ending when I'll finally be where I belong, or if I'm there already. On the other hand, decades of diligent practice of those magic mantras has left me not caring much about where I'll end up anymore.

I'm satisfied with life, and I have a strong sense of belonging that transcends the events of this fake-out world. So when things slow down enough for me to think, I realize I'm happy. What more could anyone want?

Buddha never tried to fix the world, or even the people. He just wanted to alleviate suffering by helping people shift their awareness. Living in the moment, appreciating what we have, not making happiness dependent on any external thing, and always doing our best with what we're given is the stuff happy endings are made of.

This world is on the verge of some marvelous major changes. On the other hand, our collective lack of need for any outward change is probably what will tip the scale and bring about the biggest, most personal ones. The day we take that leap of faith and follow our hearts without any expectations, giving all we have for family and friends, strangers, and enemies... That's the day we'll begin to see the old world in the rear view mirror. As we look up from tending our own little gardens, suddenly we'll find that the whole world has been magically transported to Happy Ever After Land.

We don't have to force it. We can just blast off anytime. Contrary to what we've been told, there are no tasks to complete and no enemies to defeat.

"The best way to win a war," according to Sun Tzu, *"is to let your enemy defeat himself."*

Someone else once said, *"Give 'm enough rope, and he'll hang himself."* All that anger and aggression has to go somewhere. Remove their target and watch what happens. The enemy's own fires will consume them.

When you get past the fake-outs, you realize that no singular person or group is ever our enemy. Life certainly isn't the enemy. Everyone suffers through life to some degree, but that suffering has taught us well. Those lessons were blessings, and so the suffering must also have been a blessing. Just being part of life has brought blessings to our path: flowers, children, and little successes along the way, which we eventually realize to be great rewards!

An ending is one side of the coin; the flip side is a beginning, and the coin of life is perpetually flipping. *Around and around it goes, and where it stops, no body knows.*

Endings almost always surprise us. We're surprised again when we find a new beginning. Everyone wants to think things will always be the same. Even when they aren't all that great, we cling to the joys of familiar situations.

Still, eventually things change. Kids leave home with all the *errors* of their parents in mind, anxious to create something really different on their own. We take our best shot and we learn.

Our potential is infinite, and after what we've been through, our ignorance isn't quite as infinite as it used to be. We may not know what to expect exactly. Still, I feel a glorious happy ending looming on the horizon. The path there may be slow, but after what we've been through and learned here, that path is rock solid. The tricks of life don't trap us, and the traps just don't hold us like they used to.

*To New Thought and Unity
of all levels of awareness*

33

Tricks of the Trinity

Soul, heart, and body, we thus singly name,
Are not in love divisible and distinct,
But each with each inseparably link'd.
One is not honour, and the other shame,
But burn as closely fused as fuel, heat, and flame.
–"Love's Trinity," by Alfred Austin

Once you know that everything is "inseparably link'd," you'd think that grasping that oneness would make everything simpler. Yet the game of life in this world is not so easily deciphered. It's like a three dimensional chess game.

Understanding that there's just one game prepares us to start. However, expanding our awareness to the dangers and opportunities on all levels is what finally enables us to begin playing with skill. The first necessary observation is that things that hurt us on one level may actually help us on another, so you've just got to watch what's happening on all the levels. Just when you think you've got the game down, you can suddenly become aware a strategy on a different dimension! Each of us is mind, body, and spirit. However, so is the playing field! The universe we're trying to navigate our mind, body and spirit through, also has the levels of mind, body and spirit through which we need to navigate.

The nature of life has a mind all of its own. For instance, the last hundred years or so, our minds haven't been in sync with the mind of nature. We've had different priorities, and now our bodies and the body of the world are feeling the consequences of that—less oxygen because we keep burning down the forests, and less fish in the sea because of pollution and over fishing, for instance.

Harmony demands cooperation with the spirit of the law too. Christianity divides this universal playing field into Father, Son, and Holy Ghost. Unfortunately, many Christians, just like many (or most) of everyone else just focus on one level. From this mental level, they understand the importance of every aspect of the trinity even though they miss the spiritual level perspective.

How's your relationship with Jesus?

Well, I talk with the Father, and I feel the Holy Spirit moving in my life, but Jesus, I don't know...

Wrong answer! You get no points for two out of three. The linear mind of your interrogator writes you off as a lost soul, expected to go directly to Hell. You don't pass *Go,* and you don't' collect diddly-squat!

A confrontation like this makes two important points:

1. Minds all have different fragmented focuses and fake-outs, so they don't always mesh easily, and
2. Almost everyone, no matter how misguided, understands the importance of the trinity force on some level.

American Indians think of the intelligent universal in terms of Father Sky, Mother Earth, and the Spirit that is all around, connecting us to those other two aspects. Eastern religions typically divide the universe into the functions of Creator, Maintainer, and Destroyer, which reflects the fact that our lives are always in at least one of those phases at any one time.

The trinity can also be thought of as the Positive, Negative and Neutralizing forces. These forces are at the root of all cycles on all levels that impel us through all kinds of experiences. When we're creating on one level, we may very likely be destroying something else on another level or in another aspect of our lives.

For instance, a person who devotes everything he has to his/her career may be destroying other possibilities for happiness in the process. On the other hand, sometimes when we're feeling negative about things we see, there may be something on another level, just outside our sight or comprehension, which may be working out exactly right.

In the *Phenomenon of Man,* Pere Teilhard de Chardin describes the trinity this way: "Plurality, Unity, and Energy: The three faces of matter."

One of the basic principles of matter is that "It cannot be destroyed or created." We can change matter into energy, break it up, into plurality, or combine the pieces into one thing, which is unity. Those are the choices, and each of the three faces, like the three dimensions (in a 3D world), reflect the world a little differently.

We may get a beautiful rainbow from that three-sided prism. Maybe, if we're lucky, it'll even be pretty enough to pacify us into forgetting that a clear view of everything we'd like to know, in order to make informed decisions about our lives, will probably never be in the cards.

We can understand things obscurely, or we can misunderstand them. However, complete understanding of anything is generally a mirage in the three-dimensional, trinity, worlds. I'm sure that's by design too. If we had all the knowledge we have on the other side of the veil, the whole experience of pretending to be human for the sake of developing certain qualities wouldn't work.

Increased awareness eventually results in a "game over." You rack up your points and go home. Perhaps you'll physically stick around and help others, but at that point, the tedious analysis of the trinity is only a distraction from the synthesis of the divine unity. Until that conflict is gone, the three aspects of Spirit, Mind, and Body each scream out for our attention. We have little choice but to struggle with balancing them on every level we can.

Starting from the top, the trinity of spiritual aspects is happiness, awareness, and action. Spirit is naturally happy, but attention to awareness may either infringe on that happiness or enhance it. Any action we take only magnifies this result. Throw in the trinity of mind concerns: thought, seeking (goal-oriented thought), and volition (action involving the resolutions), and you've got a quagmire of issues to deal with.

Mind evokes the authority of reason to enforce a way out of the indecision. It may tell Body that there's no time for lunch. Or it may tell Spirit that play is just out of the question. However, if it presses too hard, the happiness of Spirit retreats out of reach of Mind, leaving the body to be a slave. The simple desires of Spirit and Body want expression, but Mind just wants to pacify the others so it can get back to the real work of solving the unsolvable.

It wants to handle as much information as possible as cleverly and rationally as possible. However, there's a lot that clever rationale just can't understand on its own. Sooner or later, we just know that there's something more.

Eventually, as we come to terms with that "something more." Two realizations become inescapably clear:

1. All three aspects of Mind, Body and Spirit require equal attention; and
2. We'll probably never know all we'd like to know about any of them.

However, the big trick to the trinity isn't that the three aspects of self all need to be considered. That's just life. The real trick is that harmony between all three aspects on all three levels only really begins when we synthesize them back into one unified, driving motivation.

The Holy Ghost of Hindsight haunts us mercilessly until we resolve the conflicting demands of Mind, Body, and Spirit into the one single minded demand for life and love. Most of us here feel compelled to try every other option first on every level possible before accepting this slippery synthesis, which Mind can never really grasp.

Another reason it's so hard to get it just right is because they make us do all this **in a dualistic world** where the choices are basically "yes or no." We have a multitude of mysteries to solve! Still, and **as we march out to take on the challenge, all we take with us is an on and off switch!**

34

Doubletalk from Duality

Good and bad, right and wrong—the message is simple, and it's always true, until it isn't. When a conflict results, the inclination in the dualistic world is to externalize it. We find an enemy, so we can force the issue. We're right and they're wrong, and things proceed from there.

Conflicts that start out as a question, work their way through a mind or two, and in a marvelously creative way, you suddenly have a playing field with angry bodies on two sides advocating their position. The playing field is always a battlefield, whether or not recognized weapons of battle are used. Then, of course, *might makes right!*

That makes everyone else wrong, but at least we have order, which is good. We also have dissatisfaction, which is the fuel the dualistic world runs on. Dissatisfaction leads to upsetting the order, which is bad. But then a new order develops, and everyone has the feeling of progress, which is good.

Those who are deemed wrong may rise up against their oppressors, or they may try to change the rules, such as starting their own company, country or commune, so they can be right in their own realm—more good progress. However, in the grand scheme of things, borders create overall inefficiencies; so grander orders need to be established, along with grander elites to run them, or so the thinking goes.

‿‿

There's probably no grander example of elite, than Alexander the Great. He even had himself convinced that he was somewhat of a god. Within twelve years after taking the throne of Macedonia, he conquered most of the entire known world. His crowning achievement was the defeat of the long-standing Persian Empire, which stretched from Egypt and the Mediterranean to India and Central Asia. After using murder and mayhem to destroy the order that existed in all the countries he visited, and even killing his own aides for the glory of the Empire, he finally achieved his goal.

A new order was established. Then he died and his new order died with him. He had thrown the enormous Persian Empire into chaos, imposed order, and then after he died, finally left it in chaos again.

Isn't it interesting how all the really awful things in this world, like the 1929 Depression and Alexander are called, "Great?" Awful is great, and bad is good. It's fascinating how people seem perfectly comfortable with this doubletalk! At least the story of Alexander came with a great lesson.

Since Alexander's time, (He died 323 BC) the ones in power have become increasing proficient at controlling the masses through subtler means. "Psych ops" (psychological operations) were first launched with major success under Constantine. However, after about 1700 years, it's been fairly perfected. Today, bloody wars are only used in small doses to swipe the resources of lesser powers and to keep the people scared, and controllable. As The Great One found out, forced massive changes are unstable.

Today, control of good and bad, for our good, is an art form sculpted in the media of the mind by a pyramid of enforcement authorities. One little guy is given power over a few others, which gives him a sense of importance. The ones below him have the same arrangement. This system of control sets the order all the way from the misty Mount Olympus of money movers, down through the President and his cabinet, to business executives, middle management, lower management, and kitchen staff.

Order is good! Still the point is that with all the levels of isolated intelligence and reliance on those above us, no one below the very top of this pyramid can know what's really going on. So no regular person can really make an intelligent decision about what's good and what isn't. We try, but the real issues such as the virtue of a world run by crooks and gangs, are simply too big to grasp, so we find ourselves compelled by more meaningless stuff such as to vote for a republicorp or demicorp representative.

Still, meaningless or not, one's value is determined by the strength of his/her convictions. Right and wrong are intangibles that are too confusing and uncomfortable for many people to deal with. However, strength is something everyone understands, and the consensus is that strength is good!

Meanwhile, from the organized brutality in the streets to the heartless war mongering and maneuvering on national levels, the quest for control and order for the "good of the people," strips everyone of their freedoms, and accumulates enemies like a snowball on a steep hill. However, just like that snowball hitting a brick wall at the end of the steep hill, something interesting is happening to the Earth and those on it. The snow ball is about to stop rolling.

Your Earth will split.

That message was channeled to us by three different reliable entities in exactly the same words. I have been working on the concept of how we are all One for decades! Knowing this has been both uplifting and a little depressing.

For much of my life, I've worked on lowering my vibrations so I'd fit into this world better. I was told by Othello, a channeled ET who seems to have a very powerful grasp on things, that it was time to stop that. Others will join me, and along with our physical world, we will split off from those who aren't so familiar with the concept of oneness.

This feels like a dangerous idea to bring into the dualistic world, where factions have always seen themselves above everyone else, and have competed for all the necessities. Even life itself has been readily sacrificed because they were on the outside of the righteous us.

However, almost everyone who is inclined to think that way won't even believe in a dimensional shift that separates people by intention and vibration. So, when the differences between the people grow to a point where the split happens, most won't realize it, and life will go on as usual.

Then, fifty years from now, I'll pull this book of the shelf, dust it off, and tell the story of the rebirth of the earth to my great, great grandchildren. I expect most of them probably won't really accept it either. I suppose I just want to go on record for having pointed out this scenario because, at some point, it will make sense of things to some people when nothing else will.

As the plan plays out, we're being tested to see if we can rise above our historic conflicts and claim a reality that's beyond the reach of the deceit we've all come to know. It's also a time when illusions are being exposed and all the subtle control over us is being revealed.

Before rising to a more enlightened perspective, before our ideas and desires can find a new order, they first need to wage war in our heads to determine their priority. Many are externalizing this, finding enemies on whom to act out this inner conflict. People are facing a balancing of the karma from all their lifetimes on Earth. Then, in a marviously magical way, Mother Earth will respond to accommodate all of the people's free will choices by "splitting" what we perceive as reality when the time comes, so both levels of consciousness can have expression.

This is the new duality—a division of the world, splitting along the lines of our expectations with people carefully separated into one of two groups. Very few need to understand this because each group will see their world continue as expected for the most part, day after day.

The only difference is that someday, people will suspiciously go missing. This will be partly covered by an excellerated rate of natural attrition as the shift approaches. However, may will notice that natural death doesn't explain all of the disappearances. This sounds far-fetched, but it's a simple matter of physics, where some will vibrate at a rate that makes them and their world invisible to others. Many, if not most, of those who go with the evolved Earth will understand this eventually, but almost no one who continues to walk on the 3D, fake-out-fed world will have any idea where the missing people went—even after they're told.

As the world splits, people who cling to their own hands-on control of things at the expense of their faith in the intelligence of the universe will perpetuate the lower world we've all come to know. On the other hand, those who can cooperate with the mystical, universal laws, which work for the good of the whole, will find themselves in harmony with their higher, unlimited potential and the higher vibrational Earth, and will eventually move out of sight of all the rest.

This principal of splitting is actually a lot more common than most of us might imagine. When we split our attention, part of us actually goes one way while another part goes in a different direction. The fact that we can only focus on one life at a time is the basis for what some people perceive as alternative lives.

Jessie (one of the three entities my wife has channeled) has told me that he exists in an energy world on the other side of our Sun, which shares the same sun but in another dimension. He's also said that at the same time that he's there, he's also running a body in our physical world, and that he was the attorney who helped my wife with her divorce.

My son is my father reincarnated, but that same soul that was my father is also doing things on the other side and watching over me now and then. We all sometimes do things on different levels at the same time. Evidently, worlds can do this too.

Mother Earth has chosen her path, but the choices of many of her children are not in harmony with that path. So, this splitting of attention of the world's inhabitants is the trigger that causes what will basically be seen as a planetary alternative life.

This new duality or polarization of the Earth's people is a liberating concept that allows us to finally see ourselves and our world as spiritual, and not be pulled down by what anyone else thinks. Not caring what others think is an easy idea, which has been advocated probably since the first person started giving advice back at the dawn of time. However, there have been psychic and psychological factors that have kept us connected. When you have to live and work among'm with no hope of that ever changing, caring what they think comes pretty naturally for several reasons.

However, all that is changing now that separation (which will become very physical in the near future) between *them* and *us* is beginning. This doesn't void the oneness principal! Actually, it's our vehicle to a better understanding of it.

We don't need to try to get others to see the light any longer. **As the evolution quickens, seeing the light and love and unity of all things isn't a matter of education anymore. It's simply a matter of choice** and karma. As miraculous synchronicity fills the lives of everyone on the planet, a cooperative relationship with this mystic intelligence is either embraced or ignored in favor of a more personal power over situations. Those who try to hold tightly onto their power and control will suddenly be faced with the lesson of their lifetime as the people they control literally disappear right out of their grasp.

As we let go, our entire world is released to rise into closer proximity to those who have helped us all along. On this dawn of our birth into a new and better world, my most sincere thanks go out to all of the guides and loved ones who support us. I'm also grateful for the path of my enemies whose attitudes and expectations are taking them slowly out of my world.

Meanwhile, finely oiled on discontent and fired up on emotional obscurities, the machine of the dualistic world keeps running faster all the time. Peace, like the pot of gold at the end of the rainbow, continues to retreat. As we're confronted with more choices we hit our "good or bad" button faster all the time. Still, we're making surprisingly little progress. In desperation, we invent a third button! Yet, hitting that new *panic button* still somehow doesn't do the trick.

So, we eventually learn to disregard those buttons and try to avoid letting others hit them too. Gradually, we realize that as long as we're in the dualistic world, we really only have two choices. We can find another way, or resolve ourselves to the way things are. We can reserve judgment and get in harmony with the Earth and our higher potential, or not.

There's a story about how the appearance of things can be deceiving and the wisdom of not reacting that goes something like this: An Indian brave runs up to his friend's father and says, "Your son has just broken the stallion he was working with, and he can ride him now. Isn't that wonderful?"

The father replies, "Maybe."

The next day, the same friend comes up to the father and says, "Your son was just thrown from his horse and has broken his leg. Isn't that terrible?"

The father replies, "Maybe."

The next day the tribe has to ride into battle. All the braves are killed except the man's son who had to say in his teepee to tend his broken leg.

We can never know how things will turn out, yet we cling to our preferences like a baby does its blanket. We play with the forces of attraction and repulsion like kids with magnets. We keep things moving, so we know the balance of peace for just the briefest period before the next pole of the dualistic magnet wins, and we all lose again.

What if we could all just meet in a field where our metal isn't so powerfully magnetized? What if we could take the oil and fire out of the machine of the dualistic world? What if we could just sit back with Kali, the destructive third of the Hindu trinity, and watch the machine grind to a stop? The movers and shakers would stumble, and their entire empire would crumble without any takers for their dualistic shell game! Would that be a *BAD* thing?

> *The new day of our Western race has just begun and, during the present sub-cycle of the Sun's march through Aquarius, we will witness...a new religion, namely, the Wisdom Religion... It will embrace and embody all that is good and true of all past ages...modern science will add to and complete the dual expressions of the One Law, One Truth, One Principal and One God in whom we live, move and have our being. It will not be a house divided against itself, embodying false doctrines, false creeds and false isms, but two poles of One truth, as negative and positive... God will be glorified by His children, and they sanctified by reason of their oneness in origin and destiny with Him. Immortality will be a realized fact in consciousness, and death will be swallowed up in victory, for all shall ultimately be saved for ever more, world without end.*

That quote was from *The Duality of Truth* by Henry Wagner, MD, first published in 1899. Writers were more dramatic back then. It's a bit corny by today's standards, but I like it!

Dr. Wagner saw it coming over a hundred years ago. "God will be glorified by His children, and they sanctified by reason of their oneness in origin and destiny.... That sounds like the end of duality as we know it to me. And its "...death will be swallowed up in victory" as people en masse realize their unlimited potential once and for all.

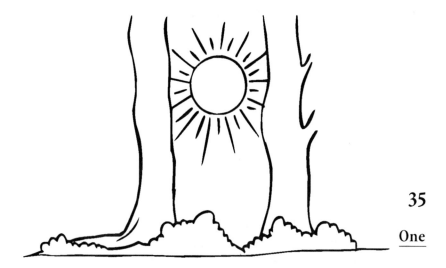

W hat if the preferences and goals of the ego could be put aside so we could finally side step injury from life's fake-outs? When we're left high and dry by disappointments, it's natural to wonder what else there could possibly be. Is the Universe trying to tell us something or maybe direct us by process of elimination? So much has been eliminated! What else is there? What are we supposed to want?

The ancients used to pass on the secret to that question with custom-tailored oral and inner revelations. It wasn't written because words can only hint at the nature of the secret. The elders had a tradition of unveiling the necessary knowledge of soul just when the time was right. However, this sort of elder vanished long ago , and the world has become darker since their passing. Some native cultures have elders and medicine men, but they've generally forgotten the answers to the questions their people no longer know to ask.

Still, the darkness of this world is all part of the divine plan where blessings hide in our loss. The beacon of soul isn't very noticeable in the light of day. However, when life looks its darkest, the night sky is absolutely covered with stars. Lines of light and love connect these stars into familiar constellations and announce the presence of kindred souls, family and our true home, in no uncertain terms.

The dualistic world may have given us two eyes, but we still only have one heart. We can work our way through life condemning people and events as bad or good, but when the day's work is done, and the sun sets on our goals and expectations, light still fills the night sky. The question is, "Would you give up your day job of anguishing over what's right and what's wrong for a chance **to know only** what's right?" Are you ready to replace your prayers beseeching the almighty, with prayers of wordless thanks?

> *God is in all.... We eat and drink his flesh and blood,*
> *because there is nothing else to eat and drink.*
> –Henry Wagner, MD from *The Duality of Truth*

He talks a lot about oneness in his dissertation on duality.

Have you ever felt a child's laughter with every cell of your body? When we feel one with others and think of them the same way we think of ourselves, we love ourselves more because if it. Worry and wonder are replaced with knowing, and everyone knows each other because we're all family.

We're all part of the same heart. When we speak from that heart, we speak the same language. Whether we're lion or lamb, something deep in all of us recognizes love when faced with it, and we all feel its joy and beauty the same. We relax into its warmth and are guided by its light as we wind our way through the dark woods of the dualistic world. Opportunity may tempt and danger may threaten. Still, we hold stoically steady with a hope and a prayer, and a heart captivated by one overriding, overwhelming love for it all.

36

The Journey Home

As we come out of the woods into the clearing, the memory of mirages still fresh in our minds, apprehension begins to take grip. How are we supposed to know what to do without the boundaries of good and bad? What are we supposed to do and how are we to know if we're still on the right track?

One reassuring sign is the instant answering of our concerns by a loving presence whose protection seems to surround us even as his reply somehow comes from within:

> *If a thought causes you fear, or if it feels bad, you've slipped back into the fake-out of the dualistic worlds—the shadow lands of conflicting concerns and "evil" forces.*

He didn't say anything about *good* forces, and that was reassuring too. The knowledge of *good* is a matter of personal experience, and we wouldn't be going home if we didn't have a lot of that. So as we plod along, away from the shadowy worlds, we contemplate what was really happening there.

When we really look into the shadows and see things for what they are, we only see our own creations, which reflect our curiosity and ignorance. Like a crazy house of mirrors, that reality can be funny or scary, depending on how much we really believe the reflection. What a strange trip we've taken on spaceship Earth!

We traded in our God-given capacity for knowing, for the ability to question and find out what's real for ourselves. We each explore in our own way, and we each lose control in our own way, looking for the shock that will shift our attention back to a soul based way of life.

This is when we begin listening more carefully and begin to see what soul sees. We learn to know what it knows, not for the purpose of changing the world, but to better belong to it below as we do above.

There are a lot of fake-outs all around, but God is in everything and everyone, and his/her agents are watching to see what we focus on. God knows when we find the task more important than the person or the trauma more appealing than trust and happiness.

When I was three or four years old, I asked my dad why we were here on Earth. He smiled and instantly answered, *"To help make other people happy."*

I was impressed he knew the answer without giving it much thought, and I really liked that answer! Fifty years later, I still haven't heard a better one.

Soul is free, happy, and anxious to share its pure love and joy! Learning to see what soul sees takes us on the journey home to claim our divine birthright of unlimited potential. The path is easy now, pulled onward by the dazzling light, the sparkling scenery, and the hum of love in the air.

We travel past questions and concerns to that peaceful spot in the heart where satisfaction is complete. We set up camp and are content to sit, warming our hands and feet around the fire. Smiles shine from every face and perfect harmony fills the air as we realize we can finally breathe a sigh of relief. We've made it.

We know now what's in the darkness of the woods. So, all desire to explore them is gone. We're safe and secure at home, and the lessons of the Fake-out world are finally complete.

~·~

About the Author

Hunt Henion spent over forty years trying to understand the workings of life. First, he was initiated into Transcendental Meditation. Then he practiced Buddhism; then studied Eckankar, "the religion of the light and sound of God," serving as a member of their clergy for six years. He finally earned his PhD in Religious Studies. Still, he never got all his questions answered until he met and married a woman who channels.

Once, in channeling, he was told that he was the crazy old man who was Cervantes's model for Don Quixote. That triggered a flood of past life memories. Hunt's appreciation for Quixote's perspective and his desire to set the record straight about that character resulted in the writing of *The Don Q Point of View.*

When Henion asked more specific questions about his past and the history and future of mankind, he got a unique perspective on that too. These insights are the subject of *Looking, Seeing & Knowing.*

After being blessed with all this insight and perspective, Henion went back to his first manuscript, *The BIG Fake-Out,* which was simply a documentation of all of life's illusions, and rewrote it (winning a Reader View's book of the year award) as this book, *The Big Fake-Out, the Illusion of Limits.*

All three of these books are different aspects of the perspective that grew after meeting Danna and having regular channeling sessions. They all tell spiritual stories from his life and past lives, and they all reveal hidden truths in uniquely heart warming ways.

Printed in the United States
146041LV00005B/1/P

9 780982 205433